ID0983424

Managing Your Own Money

A Financial Guide for the Average Wage Earner

JAMES F. TUCKER

DEMBNER BOOKS
New York, NY

To the
FEDERAL RESERVE BANK OF RICHMOND
"I just love this place"

Dembner Books
Published by Red Dembner Enterprises Corp., 80 Eighth Avenue, New York, N.Y.
10011
Distributed by W. W. Norton & Company, Inc., 500 Fifth Avenue, New York, N.Y.
10110

Completely revised and expanded edition of Personal Money Management (1984).

Library of Congress Cataloging in Publications Data

Tucker, James F., 1924–
    Managing your own money.

    Includes index.
    1. Finance, Personal. 2. Investments. I. Title.
HG179.T816 1988   332.024   87-30594
ISBN 0-042637-00-3

Contents

⟩

Preface

Many individuals and families who suffer financial strain on their present income could be enjoying a significantly higher standard of living on this same income. The problem is their failure to properly manage the money they have. Most of the individuals and families in this predicament have little formal training in managing financial resources, and lack the money needed to hire professional assistance. They want to do a better job in managing their income and improving their financial and economic outlook, but they just have not found the opportunity to do so within the time available and at a price that they can afford.

The major objective of this book is to show these individuals and families how they can improve their financial and economic well-being simply by managing their current income with greater skill. Because most of these people are only average wage earners, they are practically ignored by the literature on money management, by the institutions and firms that offer money management services, and by people who claim to be money management professionals. This book recognizes that average wage earners need and can perhaps profit more than anyone else from training in personal money management at a reasonable cost. It tries to present this training in a way that should give them confidence in achieving their financial goals.

It is assumed that the main audience for this book is wage earners not only with very modest resources, but also with very little experience in financial matters, particularly investments. With this in mind, the discussion in this book is presented at a beginner's level and contains no sophisticated mathematics or suggestions for engagement in complex or risky financial exercises. To be sure, there are some suggestions for earning money on present income. However, none of these suggestions is designed to make the individual rich overnight. The idea is to demonstrate how an average wage earner can use many of the same money management principles employed successfully by business firms, and by people with higher incomes with advice from so-called experts in personal money management.

This book is designed to serve as a guide to personal money management and as a handbook on financial affairs. Its contents are intended to provide advice for a family handling current financial affairs, as well as a long-term reference work on the basic principles of personal finance.

All of the discussion in the book represents the philosophy, opinions, and recommendations of the author. No part of the discussion is intended to reflect the philosophy, opinion, or recommendations of the author's primary employer, the Federal Reserve System. The names used in this volume are fictitious and have no relation to persons living or dead.

I am indebted to a number of persons for their assistance in bringing this book to fruition. However, I owe a special debt of gratitude to my secretary, Peggy M. Wood, for her excellent stenographic skills, and to my administrative assistant, Barbara W. Garber, for her expertise and patience in managing the overall effort.

James F. Tucker
Richmond, Virginia

1 ·

Basics Of Managing Your Own Money

During the month of June 1987, a local newspaper carried four stories that should have attracted the attention of all persons with responsibility for managing their own financial affairs. These stories reported or described the following developments:

• The Supreme Court ruled that brokerage firms may block customers from bringing fraud suits in federal courts if the customers sign an agreement beforehand with the firms to submit all disputes to **arbitration**. The customer in this case sued the brokerage firm, charging that the firm defrauded him of $560,000 by conducting excessive trading in his account. Although the customer lost his $560,000 in savings, the brokerage firm made approximately $200,000 in commissions from the securities in the customer's account.

When the customer agreed to settle disputes between the brokerage firm and himself by arbitration, he did not realize that the arbitration panel would consist of other brokers or people employed in the securities industry. The panel decided that the brokerage firm did not defraud the customer, but merely made some unfortunate trades with the customer's funds. In the final

---

• **arbitration:** an agreement between two parties that a dispute will be settled by a third party, and that the decision of the third party will be binding on both disputants.

analysis, the customer lost his $560,000 in savings, and the brokerage firm gained over $200,000 in additional income.[1]

• A well-known business and public figure pleaded guilty to operating an uninsured and unregistered bank in the British West Indies. He allegedly recruited investors with the promise that the bank was insured and its funds would remain in the United States. But the bank, which was unsupervised by federal regulators because it was not registered, lost all of its assets in an oil lease swindle, resulting in a loss of $4.4 million for the investors.[2]

• After her husband's death, a widow turned over $130,000 from life insurance benefits to a financial planner to invest. The earnings from this investment were to constitute her only source of income. Some months later the monthly payments from the investment earnings suddenly stopped. She and other investors learned that the financial planner had been using their money to repay old investors. The widow was finally forced to sell her home because she could not make the mortgage payments.[3]

• The owner of a small automobile repair shop thought that he had found a high-yield investment when he bought into a **commodities market** pool in his home town. He was quoted as saying "I was convinced it was a good thing. I put in practically everything I had saved." He and 160 others turned over a combined $1.5 million to a citizen of the same town and supposedly a friend of many of the other investors.

This trusted citizen lost most of the investors' money on the Chicago commodities market and disappeared about nine months after receiving the funds from his home town friends. He was finally caught and arrested in a neighboring state. An audit showed that he had lost more than $900,000 in the commodities

---

• **commodities market:** a market in which there is active trading of twenty-five or so commodities, many of which are agricultural products such as corn, cotton, and soybeans. The commodity itself is not traded. What *is* traded are contracts for the future delivery of these products.

market. About $650,000 was recovered from frozen bank accounts and from the sale of property, vehicles, and office furnishings owned by the trusted citizen. A federal judge ordered that the investors get thirty-eight cents on each dollar that they invested.[4]

These four stories illustrate the problems people can experience when they have little or no knowledge about managing their own money. In the situation in which the Supreme Court ruled against the investor and in favor of the broker, the investor certainly could have done no worse had he overseen the investment of his own funds. With some training in managing his own money, he may have decided to invest some of his savings in stocks, and to use a broker to assist with this investment. However, the training would have enabled him to make his own selections in buying and selling stocks, rather than entrust all of these decisions to the broker. In the second situation, the investors could have avoided the loss of their $4.4 million by having an elementary knowledge about insured banks. In the third situation, the widow could have profited from a knowledge of how to invest her own funds in investments that are safe and yield a reasonable rate of return. In the fourth situation, the owner of the repair shop and his fellow investors would not have lost sixty-two cents on every dollar of their investment if they had learned enough about some of the more common types of investments available to persons with their resources.

A reasonable amount of training in personal money management would have enabled the individuals in the aforementioned situations to avoid the problems they experienced with investments; moreover, the skills learned in this training provide other kinds of advantages and benefits for the household's financial affairs. In your household, for example, these benefits would include organization of financial records in the home, greater awareness of developments in the economy, more confidence in your financial future, better communication and relations among members of the household on financial matters, increased ability to understand financial policies and to communicate with representatives of various financial institutions and government, and less dependence on other people for direction and guidance in financial affairs.

* * *

Before embarking on personal money management, you need to know precisely what personal money management is, the factors that make it necessary, and the base that must be established in the household before any efforts at personal money management begin. In brief, personal money management is planning, analyzing, and controlling your household's financial affairs in a manner that will secure the maximum benefit from its financial resources. It is a continuing process to further the economic interests of the household.

Planning

Planning is a key element in any type of management, and it is especially crucial to personal money management. If you are coordinating or if you have primary responsibility for managing money in your household, you should ensure that broad financial goals are set for the family; that the tools of personal money management are available; that there are strategies for such activities as saving, spending, and investing; and that some procedure is established for monitoring the progress of the plans. To illustrate the value of planning, let's assume that you have a semiannual real estate property tax of $540 due on June 1, with a 9 percent penalty if you pay late. Would it be appropriate for you to invest your last $1,000 in savings in a seven-year **Treasury note** on May 1, knowing that these notes are trading at eight percent in the current securities market?

As a key element in personal money management, planning is heavily dependent on forecasting, or the ability to "look ahead." In business, just about all of a firm's operations are related in some way to a forecast. Forecasting is just as important to the financial affairs of a household, because without some idea of what future income, expenses, interest rates, tax payments, and other factors might be,

---

• **Treasury notes:** intermediate-term coupon-bearing U.S. Treasury securities having initial maturities of two to ten years and issued in denominations of $1,000 or more.

the objectives and goals of personal money management cannot possibly be achieved.

Analyzing

Analyzing is the act of separating a factor into various components, examining each component, and then relating the component back to that factor. There are several factors in personal money management, and each of them has components that may be subdivided further. It is important that you, the money manager, know all the different factors of a financial activity and their subdivisions when a decision has to be made on that activity, and know how to examine each component for its possible effect on the activity. An example is deciding whether to buy **municipal bonds**, or to buy **corporate bonds**, which carry a much higher **coupon rate**. One of the key components in this situation would be the relative safety of each of these types of bonds. Indeed, if the municipal is a **revenue bond** and the corporate bond is a **debenture**, you might want to look into the safety factor very carefully. The net yield would be another important component. Because the interest earnings from municipal bonds are exempt from all federal and state income taxes, and the earnings from corporate bonds are not, you would have to examine your income tax bracket to determine which of the two bonds would provide you with the higher net yield.

Much of the analysis required in personal money management

---

* **municipal bonds:** interest-bearing obligations of a state or of any political subdivision of a state such as a town, county, or city.
* **corporate bonds:** interest-bearing debt instruments or IOUs issued by a business corporation.
* **coupon rate:** the interest rate specified on the bond certificate and on interest coupons attached to a bond.
* **revenue bond:** bond for which the interest and the return of principal is payable from and secured by stated and expected revenues from a specific project or group of projects.
* **debenture:** an unsecured, long-term certificate of debt issued by a company against its general credit rather than against a specific asset or mortgage.

calls for the search and examination of data, some of which are mathematical in nature. You need only be able to add, subtract, multiply, and divide to analyze these data appropriately. However, you should be prepared to spend a reasonable amount of your time doing this, because the thoroughness of your efforts could result in significant financial gains or losses to your household.

Controlling

Controlling is the very heart of personal money management, because control assures the proper relationship among a household's income, expenses, **assets**, debts, and **net worth**. It is important, for example, for the household money manager to examine constantly the relationship between the percentage change in the household's income and the percentage change in the household's payments on various debts, such as mortgage payments, car loans, and installment loans on household furnishings. There may also be good reason to note when the expenditure on an item in the budget threatens to exceed a reasonable amount. For example, is it possible that the family's financial position is being jeopardized by the purchase and maintenance of too many expensive cars?

YOUR HOUSEHOLD AS A BUSINESS FIRM

You ought to recognize by now that the aforementioned functions— namely planning, analyzing, and controlling—are the same functions that are usually associated with managing a business firm. In other words, the kinds of training and skills needed to manage the financial affairs of a household are the same as those required to manage the affairs of a business firm. In a way, this comparison should come as no surprise, because there are many households

---

- **assets:** any owned properties or rights that are available for the payment of an obligation. They include cash and readily marketable securities held as investments, other items considered the equivalent of cash, accounts receivable, merchandise inventory, etc.
- **net worth:** the difference between the assets and debts (liabilities) of a person or household.

today in which the level of income and expenditures is greater than that of some small businesses. Also, many households and business firms have the same kind of expenses and similar objectives. For example, most businesses buy equipment, supplies, utilities, and insurance, and pay taxes. Doesn't your household buy the same things and also pay taxes? Many businesses also invest in operations or firms other than their own, and one of their objectives is to improve their financial condition each year. Shouldn't your household do the same thing and have the same objective?

The functions of management are practically the same for every type of organization with well-defined objectives and goals; thus persons with the responsibilities of management should have similar training regardless of the kind of organization they are managing. In some instances, the training may be acquired in a formal setting—perhaps through enrollment in an educational institution. In other instances, adequate training may be acquired informally—for example, through reading and understanding various kinds of literature.

WHY YOU MAY NEED PERSONAL MONEY MANAGEMENT

Personal money management is necessary to improve your financial status or to keep your financial status from being substantially lowered. The additional income produced through good personal money management can be used to raise your standard of living by enabling you to buy more goods and services, or to secure money to replace your regular income in case you fall victim to one of the following:

1. loss of your regular job;
2. reduction in your wages or salary due to a reduction in your work hours;
3. reduction in your regular income as a result of taking a lower-paying job.

Many of us do not show an interest in learning personal money management because we don't want to be accused of "always looking for more money." We forget that this "more money" might become our "only money" if our job is eliminated, our work hours are reduced, our employer goes out of business, or we are forced to retire early on reduced benefits.

Another key point is that personal money management is a skill that can be used "offensively" as well as "defensively." As used in this context, these two terms are not meant to describe operations or tactics that are the opposite of each other. "Offensively" in this discussion means making a gain beyond present position or status; "defensively" simply refers to avoiding any loss in present position or status.

Most of us would prefer to think that we would use personal money management offensively. The object of offensive personal money management is to produce income over and above your current salary. Regular salary raises are expected to help you achieve part of this goal. But we know that additional income from sources other than salaries can help to achieve the goal much faster. Thus, the need for personal money management should be very apparent. You cannot count on getting that winning lottery ticket or that lucky hit on a slot machine in Atlantic City or Las Vegas. You can only count on your own resources and on the training that will enable you to make the most from these resources.

On the other hand, you should not become so eager to use personal money management offensively that you ignore the need to use it defensively when certain circumstances exist. These circumstances would include situations in which the immediate problem for the household is not how to increase its income, but how to lessen the impact of a decrease in its income. Such a decrease could result from a change in employment, an increase in inflation, or a layoff. When such developments occur, personal money management can be used to maintain household income at or near its current level so that members of the household will not be forced to lower their standard of living.

WHAT IS THE MANAGEMENT PROCESS?

The management process is making decisions based on an examination of choices. The members of every household face an array of personal money management choices every minute of the day. For example, you and the members of your household must decide on such matters as wants vs. needs, durable vs. nondurable goods, tangible goods vs. services, buy vs. rent, investing vs. **remaining liquid**, short-term vs. long-term investments, and spend vs. save. Pursuing any of these particular options requires money. Since few households have sufficient sums of money to allow each member of the family to do all he would like to do, choices must be made. You should always keep in mind that a *choice is made even when the final decision is to do nothing.*

Making a decision is not a problem in itself. The problem is making the best decision or the right choice. When this necessitates spending money, for example, the right choice is the one that results in the greatest economic advantage. Experience shows that you have a better chance of making the right choice when you recognize that a choice should be made and that you have a reasonable amount of skill in making the choice.

In personal money management, the basic skill in making choices is knowing how to conduct a cost vs. benefit analysis. Cost/benefit analysis, in its simplest form, is calculating all of the costs associated with various choices and comparing them with all of the benefits associated with those choices. The best or right choice is the one in which the benefits exceed the costs associated with that choice by the greatest margin. To illustrate the need for such cost/benefit analysis, let's review the following situation:

> Currently, Mr. Gipson has a wife and two school-age children, a $50,000 mortgage on his home, a very modest salary from a job that he has held for twelve years, and a very small amount of savings in a passbook account. He also has $50,000 that he inherited just a few days ago and visions of now achieving at least two of the objectives that he set for himself during the past several years: a debt-free home for his family in the event of some sudden misfortune on his part, and a portfolio of investments that would provide a significant amount of extra income to supplement his salary.

It is clear that Mr. Gipson has two worthy objectives, and it is

• **remaining liquid:** having assets in cash or in a form that can be converted to cash immediately and easily.

also clear that there are several alternatives available to him for achieving either one of these objectives or part of both. For example, to assure the debt-free home, he can use all of the $50,000 to pay off the remaining mortgage balance or he can purchase mortgage insurance and invest most of the $50,000 with a view toward using some of the investment income to pay the new insurance premium. To accumulate the portfolio of investments that would provide a significant amount of extra income for the household, he could invest the $50,000 in long-term Treasury securities, with a view toward using the interest earnings to supplement the household's current income and then instructing his wife to liquidate all of these highly marketable securities to pay off the home mortgage in the event of his untimely death. Mr. Gipson must make a decision, and he has a better chance of making the right decision for his household if he conducts a cost/benefit analysis on each of the available alternatives. To conduct this analysis, he needs information on all of the alternatives, and most, if not all, of this information can be obtained through an understanding of the components of personal money management.

While ability to make a cost/benefit analysis is the basic skill needed for personal money management, you must supplement this skill with additional information and guidance in order to complete your training in personal money management. Training in personal money management is a continuing process, and it can be very time-consuming. But as George Sullivan concludes in his book, *The Boom Is Going Bust: The Threat of a National Scandal*: "In many cases, money today is easier to earn than it is to manage, and it is unrealistic that an individual devotes years to preparing himself for a good paying job but scarcely any time at all to the use and management of what he plans to earn."

WHY SETTING FINANCIAL GOALS MUST BE THE FIRST STEP

Before embarking on what should be a lifelong program in personal money management, you and your family should establish financial goals. For any undertaking, exercise, or operation to be meaningful for you, you should have in mind a clear set of goals that you would like to achieve. The goals may be short-term or long-term; they may change with the times or circumstances. However, there is one factor that should be constant, namely the element of realism. Every goal—regardless of its unique features—should be attainable.

Many financial goals are very broad and are taken for granted in most households. These include the following: (1) having adequate food, clothing, and shelter; (2) accumulating enough money to educate the children; and (3) living comfortably during retirement. While such goals are admirable, they are not specific enough to guide the actions and analysis of personal money management.

At the outset of a plan for personal money management, the entire family should discuss and decide upon the family's financial goals. Some of these goals may be very short-term, such as accumulating enough funds to purchase a single item for cash. These items frequently include televisions, appliances, and vacation trips. In some instances, the goal might not be to purchase a single tangible item, but rather to attain a specified financial status, such as remaining free of debt other than a home mortgage, or always having a certain amount of cash in a checking or savings account. An increasing number of families are setting goals that are related to an increase in wealth through sources other than their regular employment.

In establishing various goals for personal money management,

Figure 1–1. Goals for Personal Money Management

GOAL: To generate additional family income from savings and investments

OBJECTIVES	METHOD OF ACCOMPLISHMENT	TIME
To generate enough extra income to buy one household appliance	Start a regular savings program by depositing an amount from each pay check	1 Year
To generate sufficient income to pay one-month's mortgage on the house	Accumulate sufficient savings and earnings from savings to buy at least two T-notes or T-bonds	3–4 Years
To generate approximately 1/5 of the family's income from earnings on investment	Reinvesting most of the earnings from investments	10–15 Years

you and your family should recognize the importance of setting a schedule for achieving the goals. This suggests that objectives leading to each goal should be set when the goals are established, and that a time frame should be determined for meeting each of the objectives. This time frame ought to be based on a combination of experience and best estimates for the future. Above all, the time frame should anticipate successive changes in the life cycle of the family, which in turn will have a crucial bearing on the financial plans of the family. (See figure 1–1.)

Generally, the family's costs are lower during the brief period before children become a part of the family. Costs rise as the children are born and grow up, and costs reach a peak during the children's high school and college years. As children become adults and leave the household, the family's costs begin to decline. (See figure 1–2.)

Figure 1–2. The Family Life Cycle

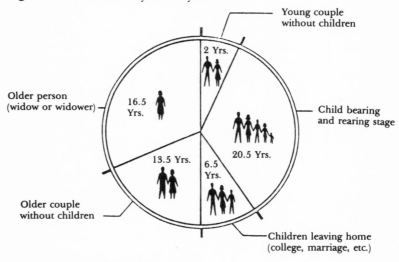

THE FAMILY LIFE CYCLE

When the family costs are at first lower, then higher, and then lower during the years of retirement, family income is at first lower, then higher, then lower during retirement. These cost and income streams, however, do not flow precisely as close together as the changes indicate. The initial phase of the family cycle, when costs are lower, is a very short period in most instances. The next phase, the cycle that includes childbearing, high school, and college, is a relatively long period. Although family income usually rises steadily during this cycle, it is often insufficient to meet the rising costs in the early-to-middle years of the cycle. This situation is certainly likely to exist if the family has two or more children attending college or professional school at the same time.

Income is one of the most important determinants of the family's living standard. The family that reaches more of its social and economic goals is one that develops a plan for spending its income, and then controls and adjusts its plan as needed. The family should be realistic about its current and future income, and should plan its expenditures to achieve the most satisfying standard of living during each phase of its life cycle.

While most families progress through the cycles discussed previously, each family is still unique in many ways. How the family lives is influenced by its values, goals, income, education, stage in the family's life cycle, and geographic location. It is important that your family ascertain its priority of values with regard to health, knowledge, economic security, leisure, and comfort during each phase of the family cycle.

IS PERSONAL MONEY MANAGEMENT FOR EVERYONE?

The answer to the above question is a resounding "yes." The following excerpts from an article in a local newspaper provide support for this conclusion.

"Lack of money is an underlying cause of why welfare parents physically neglect their children, according to a study done by the State Department of Social Services.

But equally as important, the study found that parents lack *money management skills* and adequate knowledge of how to care for their children.

Lack of knowledge of adequate child care was noted in 62 percent of non-ADC cases, while *poor money management was cited in 50 percent*, the study said.

The board adopted the department's recommendations that local welfare departments provide parents with counselling and *training in areas such as money management*, problem resolution and child development."[5]

Most, if not all, people today agree that personal money management should be practiced by everyone who has income and expenses, regardless of the level of these two factors. It is perhaps safe to say that most people today, in fact, do practice personal money management to some extent. However, the important questions are: Do they know the purposes of personal money management? Do they have goals for their personal money management, along with strategies for achieving these goals? And finally, can they point to any results of their personal money management?

Many families engage in a lifelong race of "watching expenses" and "getting more money." But they have no goals and have no strategies for winning this lifelong race. This chapter has discussed the need to watch expenses and get more money, but it has recommended that those actions be pursued in an organized fashion, with a set of goals in view. In other words, personal money management is not designed to take these families out of the lifelong race. It should, however, give them a better chance at winning it.

2·

Tools Of Personal Money Management

All skills involve the use of tools, and the skill of management is no exception. The most important component of management skill is decision-making, and although many of the tools used in this skill are not subject to patents or produced as different models from year to year, they are viewed as instruments, implements, and devices. Like all tools, they experience changes in quality from time to time, and should be reviewed periodically for their effectiveness in helping to accomplish the assigned tasks.

As a manager of your household's financial affairs, you will find that many of your tools are right at your finger tips at little or no extra cost. Other tools, however, might require extra efforts to obtain, and in some cases, additional training to use.

This chapter does not attempt to list or describe all of the tools of personal money management, nor does it attempt to categorize the tools by availability. However, based on this discussion, you should be able to recognize those tools that are readily available to you, as compared with those that will involve further action to obtain.

INFORMATION

For any manager of an ongoing organization, information is the most important tool needed for making decisions. This includes information generated within the organization, as well as information emanating from outside the organization. Starting with setting goals and continuing through the realization of these goals, the need to obtain, analyze, and use money management information is imperative. Having this information does not guarantee success. However, the failure to get information leaves the chances for success entirely up to luck and often reduces the chances for success to almost zero. As indicated in chapter 1, active personal money management sharpens the decision-making skills needed for one to reach rational conclusions when faced with several choices. By using the right information about your financial affairs, you can use these skills to their maximum potential.

As an individual seeking training in personal money management, you should not consider this training as complete after reading and understanding the topics discussed in this book. There are other specialized topics, such as buying food, automobiles, and health care that are not discussed here, but that can play a crucial role in personal money management. As a matter of fact, you should seek information about *anything* you spend money on. This would ensure that every dollar expended is subject to a cost/benefit analysis, and that you have all the information needed for that analysis.

Before seeking information on the specialized topics associated with personal money management, you should learn the key terms used in discussing these topics. This will help guide you through your reading on these topics, and also aid you in communicating with people who may become involved in your financial affairs. For example, before seeking specialized information on investments available at commercial banks, saving and loan associations, credit unions, and money market mutual funds, you should acquaint yourself with such terms as **accrued interest, amortize** and **annual percentage rate (APR)**.

After you become familiar with various key terms and concepts, you should benefit from a considerable amount of information in the

---

- **accrued interest:** interest earnings accumulated on a financial interest-bearing asset.
- **amortize:** to reduce a debt through regular and equal payments.
- **annual percentage rate (APR):** the cost of credit over a full year, expressed as a percentage, reflecting all costs of the loan as required by the Truth in Lending Act.

general media appearing under such headings as *personal investments, personal finance, consumer information,* and *consumer views.* This information is aimed at the average person and is usually very current. In many cases, the information focuses on one particular option for investing, saving, or buying. Your task, in such cases, is to find out about other options and then compare them to decide which are best for you and your family. Also, don't underestimate the value of various types of information. Grocery advertisements can have just as much of an impact on the management of the family's resources as inside tips on the stock market.

Sources of Information

Fortunately, the sources of information on personal money management are growing, and many of them are inexpensive. Larger daily newspapers, for example, carry information on a variety of financial topics. Most newspapers carry stock market quotations, quotations on Treasury securities, and a regular column for consumers. Newspapers like the *Washington Post*, the *New York Times*, and the *Richmond Times Dispatch* are noted for their news and columns on investments and personal money management. A thorough reading of the financial section of most daily newspapers can provide you with timely information on such items as mortgage rates, changes in tax rules, changes in interest rates on savings, and future offerings of stocks, bonds, and government securities.

If you read some of the information carefully enough to apply your analytical skills, you might be able to do your own forecasting of financial developments. For example, if you regularly buy Treasury bills as a short-term investment, then you are aware that these securities are sold at **auction** every Monday at the regional Federal Reserve banks (and the Bureau of Public Debt in Washington, D.C.). The **yield** on the securities is not announced until after they

---

- **auction:** the sale of Treasury securities by the U.S. Treasury on a bid basis.
- **yield (or rate of return):** measurement of the profitability of an investment; it is usually per year on the amount invested; often referred to as return on investment.

are sold. In most instances, you do not even know the direction that the yield will take—that is, up or down from the previous week. If you read the financial pages of your newspaper consistently, however, you might find information to help you to predict at least the direction of the yield on Treasury bills scheduled to be sold at the next auction. To illustrate further, whenever the Federal Reserve changes the **discount rate**, the announcement of the changes is usually the subject of an article in every local newspaper the next day (see exhibit 2–1). On the Monday following the story, Treasury bills are offered at auction to the public. If the announced change in the discount rate is an increase, more than likely the rate on the Treasury bills will increase. If the change is a decrease, usually the rate on the Treasury bills will decrease. To illustrate this, in the Treasury Auction on the Monday following the decrease in the discount rate shown in exhibit 2–1, rates on Treasury bills decreased as follows:

Rates on Treasury Bills

Dates	*3-Month*	*6-Month*
	%	%
August 18, 1986	5.65	5.65
August 25, 1986	5.32	5.35

As you can see from the above illustration, the rates on both three-month and six-month Treasury bills showed a decrease at the Monday auction of August 25, following the decrease in the discount rate announced on the previous Thursday, August 21.

Weekly news magazines, such as *Business Week, Time, Newsweek,* and *U.S. News and World Report,* and monthly magazines, such as *Black Enterprise,* also devote regular columns to information on personal money management.

Of course, there are magazines that specialize in information on personal money management. The best known of these are *Changing*

• **discount rate:** the rate of interest that Federal Reserve Banks charge financial depository institutions that wish to borrow funds from these Banks.

Exhibit 2–1   Thursday, August 21, 1986

Fed drops discount rate to 5.5%

Board's attempt to stir economy may not be last this year

By Martin Crutsinger
The Associated Press

WASHINGTON—The Federal Reserve Board is trying once again to stimulate a sluggish economy by slashing a key bank lending rate, and many financial analysts are predicting it won't be the last effort made this year.

The Fed announced that effective today it is cutting its discount rate, the fee it charges for loans to U.S. banks, from 6 percent to 5.5 percent, the lowest it has been since August 1977.

Economists predicted the Fed action would be followed immediately by a cut in the prime lending rate charged by banks. They said other business and consumer interest rates, including mortgage rates, would fall as well.

Analysts predicted that in addition to the prime rate falling to 7.5 percent, mortgage rates would dip below 10 percent, down almost 4 percentage points from the highs of last year.

Several interest rates already have fallen to the lowest levels in nine years, and the Fed action is expected to accelerate that trend.

The Fed hopes the lower interest rates will stimulate consumer and business spending and provide the momentum to get the stalled U.S. economy moving again.

The central bank announced its decision yesterday, a day after the government revealed that the overall economy, as measured by the gross national product, slumped to an annual growth rate of 0.6 percent, the weakest showing since the end of the last recession.

The GNP figure and other economic signals have raised new fears that the 44-month-old economic recovery is in danger of toppling into another recession.

The Fed action marked the fourth time this year that the central bank has cut its discount rate after disappointing news about the economy's performance. Analysts predict a fifth reduction could come in September if the economy remains in the doldrums.

"The Fed is in a month-to-month watch focusing on the domestic economy" said David Jones, an economist with Aubrey G. Lanston & Co., a government securities dealer. "As long as the economy remains flat, the Fed is prepared to push interest rates lower."

Both Jones and Allen Sinai, chief economist for Shearson Lehman Brothers, said the Fed also was interested in cutting the discount rate as a way of driving down the value of the dollar on foreign exchange markets and thus shrinking the country's disastrous foreign trade deficit.

By pushing interest rates in the United States lower, the Fed drives down the value of the dollar because foreign investors are less enthusiastic about holding U.S. investments that earn lower rates. A weaker dollar, in theory, drives up the costs of imports to Americans while lowering the price of American agricultural products and other goods on overseas markets.

The trade deficit, expected to soar to a record $170 billion this year, is blamed for the near recession in American manufacturing and farming and the disappointing growth of the past two years.

In recent days, top administration officials, including White House budget director James Miller and chief of staff Donald Regan, joined the chorus calling for Fed Chairman Paul Volcker to cut the discount rate. Many Republicans feared that a worsening economic picture would prove disastrous to GOP election chances in the fall.

Source: Richmond News Leader, Thursday, August 21, 1986.

Times, Consumer Reports, Money and *Your Moneysworth*. Other magazines like *Better Homes and Gardens, Good Housekeeping, Consumers Union Digest,* and *Consumers' Research Magazine* concentrate on consumer products and the financial services associated with these products.

Considerable information that can aid personal financial management is published by various financial institutions and public agencies. These include commercial banks, consumer affairs departments of state and local governments, and **brokerage houses**. The information often takes the form of newsletters, bulletins, or reports, and is published on a regular basis. Much of the same information is sometimes disseminated through the broadcast media.

FINANCIAL STATEMENTS AND RECORDS

After you and your family clearly identify the goals and objectives of personal money management, and after you become acquainted with the types and sources of information you will need, you should be ready to start your program by developing an initial set of records on your financial affairs. These records are a tool of money management and it is your responsibility to develop and maintain them. The first document among these records should be a statement showing the financial position of the family. This is known as a **net worth statement** and is similar to a **balance sheet**, used in business. The net worth statement should show all of the

---

- **brokerage house:** a firm, often a member of a stock exchange, that handles the public's orders to buy and sell securities. The firm charges a fee for this service.
- **net worth statement:** a financial form that lists, as of a specific date, the financial assets and liabilities of a person or household, and shows the difference between the two as the net worth.
- **balance sheet:** a statement showing the nature and amount of a company's assets, liabilities, and capital on a given date.

tangible items used by the household, debts owed to the family, and debts owed by the family to others. In addition to showing the financial status of the household at a specific time, a net worth statement can serve such purposes as:

1. providing data that may be required in a business transaction, such as applying for a loan at a bank;
2. determining whether the current homeowner's insurance policy provides adequate coverage for the present household;
3. estimating the value of a family member's **estate**, and thus an estimate of the estate tax when that family member dies;
4. providing a means of gauging the financial progress of the household when similar net worth statements are drawn up for future years.

Appropriate Data

As a starting point in collecting data for a net worth statement, you should list all of the household's assets in two groups. The first group should be designated as **liquid assets** and would include cash and anything that could be quickly converted into cash without a loss of principal. The second group should be designated as nonliquid assets and would include those items that could be converted into cash but with a possible loss in principal. As you list these nonliquid assets, you should estimate their present or market value and *not* the price paid for them. With regard to your liabilities or debts, you should list these in groups that indicate how long you have to complete repayment. Payments that are due within a year

---

- **estate:** a person's ownership and/or interest in all forms of property. Also, the financial resources and personal assets left upon the person's death.
- **liquid assets:** all real and personal property owned by a person or household that can easily be converted into cash at a readily determinable fair price.

Figure 2–1. Net Worth Statement

David and Mary Flowers and Family as of June 31, 1987

ASSETS

I. Assets—liquid:

Cash

On hand	$ 150.00
Savings accounts	850.00
Checking accounts	1,550.00
Other	150.00
Total cash	$ 2,700.00

Life insurance (cash value):	$ 3,100.00

Investments (market value):

Bonds	5,000.00
Stocks	3,000.00
Certificates of deposit	3,000.00
Vested interest in profit sharing-plan	5,000.00
Total investments	$16,000.00

II. Assets—nonliquid (market value):

House	50,000.00
Household furnishings	15,000.00
Special items (car, boat, etc.)	10,000.00
Furs, jewelry, etc.	5,000.00
Other real estate	10,000.00
Total nonliquid assets	$90,000.00

TOTAL ASSETS $111,800.00

LIABILITIES

I. Liabilities—short term:

Charge account balances	1,550.00
Installment loan balances	850.00
Taxes due	500.00
Insurance premiums owed	300.00
Total short-term liabilities	$3,200.00

II. Liabilities—Long term:

Mortgage	41,000.00
Automobile loan balance	3,800.00
Total long-term liabilities	$44,800.00

TOTAL LIABILITIES $48,000.00

NET WORTH (Total Assets minus Total Liabilities)

                                                          $63,800.00

Figure 2–2. Net Worth Statement

"Rich as Rockefeller": *Net Worth* $62.6 Million

The nation had its first glimpse into the meaning of the phrase "rich as Rockefeller" Sept. 23, 1974, when Nelson A. Rockefeller, nominated as vice president, disclosed details of his FINANCIAL status at the request of the Senate Rules Committee.

NET WORTH

As of Aug. 28, 1974 Rockefeller reported that his and his wife's total assets were $64 million. When his liabilities were deducted, Rockefeller's *net worth* on that date was $62.6 million, he said. As he itemized it:

ASSETS

Cash	$ 394,898
Cash advances	247,891
Notes receivable	1,518,270
Accounts receivable	713,326
N.Y. State Retirement Fund (contributed cost)	21,803
Securities	12,794,376
Partnership interest	157,124
Art (estimated market value)	33,561,325
Real estate	11,252,261
Furnishings	1,191,328
Automobiles, other vehicles, boats and airplanes	1,767,900
Jewelry	521,136
Coins	12,600
TOTAL ASSETS	$64,154,238

LIABILITIES

Notes payable	1,567,500
Miscellaneous accounts payable	5,513
TOTAL LIABILITIES	$ 1,573,013
NET WORTH	$62,581,225

Source: Data was compiled by the author from the *Washington Post* (9/24/74), the *Richmond Times Dispatch* (9/24/74), the *New York Times* (9/24/74), the *Wall Street Journal* (9/24/74), and the *Congressional Record* (9/74).

should be designated as **short-term** liabilities, while those debts that are payable over a period of years should be designated as long-term liabilities.

After you add the two groups of assets to get your total assets, and the two groups of liabilities for total liabilities, you should subtract your total liabilities from your total assets, which will give you your family's net worth (See figure 2–1). In most instances, you

• **short-term:** a period of one year or less.

will look favorably at the net worth figure if it represents an increase over the net worth of the previous year. If your total liabilities add up to more than your total assets, you have a negative net worth and perhaps a problem. If your net worth changes little from year to year, this is a sign that you should review the financial management in your household to determine whether your present strategy will achieve your family's financial goals.

To be meaningful, net worth must represent what the household owns as of a specific date. Thus, in drawing up a net worth statement, you should list the assets and liabilities of the household as of a specific date. This date should appear at the top of the statement.

Inventories

Developing a net worth statement is much easier when you already have a household **inventory**. You could have several inventories. These could include separate lists for such possessions as furniture; such financial assets as stocks, bonds, and certificates of deposit; face value and issuer of insurance policies; and locations of all checking and savings accounts.

Special care should be taken in devising an inventory for securities. In addition to showing the organization's name and the serial (certificate) number of the **financial instrument**, your form should have the date of purchase, the purchase price, the date of the last dividend or interest payment, and the amount of the payment.

Safekeeping of Documents

Closely associated with household inventories is the matter of safekeeping the various documents listed on the inventories. It is important, for example, to keep stock certificates, bonds, and insurance policies in a safe place—that is, safe from theft, fire, or misplacement. A safe-deposit box at a bank can provide this kind of

- **inventory:** a completed listing of all the household's assets.
- **financial instrument:** any written document or contract having monetary value or showing a monetary transaction.

safety. If it is big enough, the box may also be used for such documents as armed service records (which might entitle you to benefits at a later date); deeds and surveys of your real estate; personal papers, such as marriage and birth certificates, divorce decrees, separation and naturalization papers; titles to automobiles; and duplicate copies of various household inventories. You should not keep a will in this safe-deposit box (whether the box is in your name or joint names). A safe-deposit box is generally sealed when the owner dies and is not opened until the **executor** and the estate tax authorities can check on its contents. You may want to leave a copy of your will in your lawyer's office.

Several documents may be kept at home in a steel cabinet or in cardboard box files. Such papers may include immunization records, monthly bank statements, charge accounts statements, and a list of credit card numbers. Information needed for filing income taxes should also be kept in home files. Because the Internal Revenue Service suggests that a taxpayer maintain tax records for at lease three years, it is advisable to set up separate tax files for each of the three years prior to the current year. Further, your should adopt the practice of placing every item applicable to the current year's income tax in the current year's tax file.

FISCAL OPERATIONS IN THE HOUSEHOLD

After determining the financial kickoff point for personal money management by making a net worth statement and setting up a system for keeping records and other key information, you are now ready to begin the day-to-day operations associated with personal money management. The first of these operations concerns getting and spending money. Like similar operations in most organized institutions, a specific method of receiving and disbursing money in the home should be a part of the household's overall fiscal policy. Although the term fiscal policy sounds a bit formal in discussions of

---

* **executor:** an individual appointed in a will and approved by a probate court to administer the disposition of an estate according to directions in the will.

the family budget, experience indicates that a settled and agreed-upon course of action for handling money not only reduces the likelihood of mistakes and inconsistencies, but also minimizes the potential for tension and misunderstanding among members of the household.

Direct Deposit

The first thing you should do is determine how the money becomes available to the household. Many people still think this is a simple matter of making sure that the breadwinner comes straight home with the pay check. More and more employers, however, are giving their employees the option of having their pay forwarded electronically to the employee's bank. This is called **direct deposit.**

In June 1987, the controller for the state of California said that of 25.5 million checks issued by his office last year, more than 25,000 were lost, stolen, or otherwise not received by the correct payee. These 25,000 incidents included 8,000 wage and retirement checks worth $5.4 million, and 2,000 cases of forgery—problems that direct deposit would eliminate.

If you have never used direct deposit, you may wonder how it works. It's really very simple. On payday you receive a statement confirming that your earnings have been deposited automatically into an account at your bank, savings and loan association, or credit union—whichever institution you specify to your employer. This step-saver gives you more time to do other errands or to enjoy leisure activities.

Direct deposit also:

1. allows interest earnings to start accumulating as soon as payments are automatically deposited into a savings or interest-bearing checking account;
2. provides immediate availability of your funds;
3. eliminates the risk of late payments;
4. eliminates the risk of lost or stolen checks;

* **direct deposit:** a system in which the employee's or investor's earnings are deposited directly to his or her account at a depository institution.

5. assures that your funds will be deposited in your account, even if you're too sick to go to your bank or if you are on an extended vacation.

If you don't have a regular account at a financial institution, the direct deposit option is a good reason to open one and take advantage of all the benefits described above.

As a safeguard, the use of direct deposit requires your consent in writing. Your employer or the agency that issues your funds can give you the appropriate forms. Your depository institution, your employer, or the agency issuing your funds must provide a way for you to verify the deposit of funds to your account. The verification may be issued in the form of a written notice. Otherwise, a telephone number may be provided for verbal verification.

Automatic Bill Paying

Automatic bill paying will assure that you will never be inconvenienced because of an unpaid bill that you forgot to mail. Many banks and savings and loans will pay recurring bills for you automatically—utility bills, auto payments, or mortgage payments, for example. All that is required is that you authorize the company to bill your depository institution. This service is sometimes referred to as a preauthorized transfer.

The advantages of automatic bill paying include:

1. saving on the cost of checks and the time spent writing the checks;
2. saving on the cost of postage and envelopes;
3. avoiding penalty fees incurred when the bill is not paid on time;
4. knowing that bills will be paid even when you are out of town for extended periods of time.

Although you may pay a small fee for automatic bill-paying services, the overall cost of paying your bills will probably be less. Again, as a safeguard, your authorization for automatic bill paying by your depository institution must be in writing. When this is done, you are, in effect, authorizing the billing company to collect from your depository institution. Be sure to have enough money in your account to cover the withdrawal.

Should you want to prevent a payment which you have previously authorized, you must give notification—verbally or in writing—three business days prior to the scheduled date for transfer. A verbal stop order may have to be confirmed in writing.

Other Records

Remember, your records on your various financial activities and transactions constitute the basic source of information that you need to make the best decisions for your household. While it is obvious that you should maintain records on all activities that may affect your taxes, there are other records that should be maintained just as diligently. For example, you should maintain a listing of all real estate transactions. In one of these transactions, you may have permitted the buyer of your house to assume your mortgage. If so, you are still liable for the payment of that mortgage until it is satisfied. There is also the possibility that someone can find fault with the title of a home that you previously owned and sold.

Keeping records on specific financial activities will be discussed in subsequent chapters on these activities. Nevertheless, it is important at this point to emphasize that the household's records are crucial to all of the decisions made on its financial affairs.

Household Cash

Another part of your family's fiscal policy is often referred to as "household cash," which is money that should be available for food, gasoline, allowances for the children, household supplies, entertainment and recreation, and other items for which cash is needed frequently. Experience is the best guide for arriving at a good estimate of your household's cash needs for a certain period of time—say, a week. Setting a policy on your cash needs can avert confusion and needless misunderstandings in the family.

Only one member of the household should have responsibility for writing checks for specific recurring expenditures. This will reduce such mistakes as forgetting to pay certain bills or making duplicate payments.

Again, the term fiscal policy might appear to be too formal for a single family's finances. However, besides providing the advantages already described, the arrangement suggested by this term reflects the essential systematic procedures and operations needed for successful personal money management. Money is a scarce resource for most of us. To get the maximum value from this resource, we must approach each decision in an orderly fashion, which usually means having a plan or a specific course of action.

SERVICES OFFERED BY FINANCIAL INSTITUTIONS

Even though you may have a thorough understanding of the rudiments of managing your own financial affairs, you still may feel more comfortable in seeking assistance from other sources. In some instances you *must* rely on other sources—such as the use of brokers when you want to buy and sell securities issued by a private corporation (other than those sold to employees or customers in stock purchase plans). In other situations, you might feel that a financial decision calls for the kind of in-depth research that involves more time and effort than you are willing to give. For these kinds of situations, you may well be justified in seeking assistance from outside sources. The following is a brief discussion of just one of the outside sources you might wish to consider.

Bank Holding Companies (BHCs) are now allowed by the Federal Reserve to offer members of the general public two new services, namely consumer financial counseling and tax planning/tax preparation. Through the service of financial counseling, these companies can provide you with guidance, educational courses, and instructional material on consumer-oriented financial matters, including debt consolidation, mortgage applications, bankruptcy, budget management, real estate tax shelters, tax planning, retirement and estate planning insurance, and general investment management. This service does not involve the sale of specific products or investments or the provision of portfolio investment advice or portfolio management.

The authorization to offer tax planning/tax preparation services allows BHCs to provide you and others in the general public with advice and strategies designed to minimize tax liabilities, as well as analyses of the tax implications of retirement plans, estate planning, and family trusts. Tax preparation involves the preparation of tax forms and advice concerning liability based on records and receipts supplied by the consumer-client.

FINANCIAL PLANNERS

For a fee or some type of commission on an investment product, there are individuals who will seek to plan all of your household's financial affairs. These individuals call themselves financial planners, and they operate in some instances as one-person consultants, while in other instances as members of a firm. Some firms support their planners with a highly trained staff of research analysts with expertise in such areas as taxes, pensions, insurance, corporate investments, real estate, etc.

It is difficult to pinpoint a specific set of credentials for a financial planner that would enable a household client to determine whether the planner is fully qualified to provide professional advice in financial matters. However, if you have the choice of selecting a financial planner through recommendations by close personal friends or selecting one based on your interpretation of the letters behind his or her name, you may well be advised to use the former. In her study, *Financial Planning Abuse: A Growing Problem*, conducted for the Consumer Federation of America, Barbara Roper stated that "fraud in financial planning cost Americans a half billion last year, and an equal amount may simply have been misinvested by incompetent planners."[1]

Before seeking the services of a financial planner, you ought to be sure that you truly need this kind of assistance, particularly in view of the four digit fees that most planners charge. Frankly, in a household in which the total income is less than six figures a year, the decision-makers themselves ought to be able to plan the household's financial affairs adequately by reading the literature on money management and attending various lectures and seminars on the topic whenever such sessions are available.

If after a thorough review of your situation, you are convinced that you need the assistance of a financial planner, you should be prepared to indicate the specific areas of your financial affairs that you wish to include in the plan. For example, the plan should include such crucial areas as cash management, budgeting, tax planning, retirement planning, saving, investments, and insurance needs.

There are a variety of statistics on the number of financial planners in the United States today. In the aforementioned study for the Consumer Federation of America, it was estimated that "between 250,000 and 400,000 people across the country call themselves financial planners."[2]

There are approximately 10,000 self-proclaimed financial planners registered with the Securities and Exchange Commission (SEC). By compensation, they fit into three categories as follows:

Commission.   Most of these planners are insurance agents whose earnings come from commissions on the policies that they sell. The insurance policies, of course, are a part of their recommended plan. Although most of these planners are ethical, their knowledge of other financial products is not nearly as extensive as their knowledge of insurance. Also, the mere fact that they receive a commission on one of the products that they are recommending for the plan raises the problem of conflict of interest.

Fee-Plus-Commission.   These planners charge an up-front fee to draw up the initial plan, and also receive commissions on the investment products that they recommend and sell as a part of the plan. These products include mutual funds, insurance policies, real estate partnerships, and various securities. Again, because they receive commissions on these products, their retention also raises the problem of conflict of interest.

Fee-Only.   These planners charge a single fee for drawing up a plan, and do not receive any commissions on any investment products that they recommend for the plan. These are the only financial planners that are accepted as members of the National Association of Personal Financial Advisors.

In scrutinizing a plan suggested by a financial planner, you should, among other things, make sure that the plan is presented basically in narrative that you can understand, and not all in statistics and other numbers. Also, you should assure yourself that the narrative clearly spells out the various objectives and goals of your household's financial affairs and recommends more than one way of achieving these objectives and goals.

3·
Budgeting: A Practical Approach

In the simplest terms, budgeting is allocating one's income to cover one's expenses. Budget is a term given to a plan for the allocation of income to specific expenses. Budgeting can be a very formal exercise in which the budget becomes a written plan which is adhered to rather rigidly. It can also be a process so informal that it may hardly qualify as budgeting. The important factor is that every household should have some sort of a plan for allocating the family's income and watching its expenses. Such a plan, regardless of its form, can become one of the most valuable tools in personal money management.

Among other important characteristics, budgeting forces the household to think about alternatives in spending. Budgeting facilitates a clearer view of the alternatives, helps in weighing the value of these alternatives, and in the final analysis, enables the household to make wise decisions. Of course, the whole process of allocating the household's income ensures staying within that income and helps to avoid hopeless entanglement in debt and financial worries in the future.

Experience shows that few households use a formal budgeting procedure. Many newly-married people do so because they are eager to see just what the relationship is between income and expenses in the new arrangement. After some experience, they usually resort to some type of informal budgeting.

Alternative methods exist for controlling household expenditures if you do not want to maintain a formal budget. Informal budgeting is based on keeping several separate controls, none of which is indispensable to the primary objective of the plan. However, should the overall financial plan fall short of its objectives, more of these controls should be used, and their warning signals be taken seriously. If the household is not meeting its financial objectives with informal budgeting, a formal and written budget should be adopted.

DECIDING ON A BUDGET

If you decide to develop a budget as a tactic in financial planning, you should adhere to the following four key guidelines:

1. The budget should be tailored to your individual household.
2. All members of your family should participate in developing the budget—although some members may have greater participation than others.
3. Every member of the household, including children, should understand clearly the overall budget and those parts of the budget related to his or her interest or responsibility.
4. The records should be kept simple.

Your Budget

There is no "average" budget for everyone. Published information on budgets is in the form of percentages, averages, and formulas, and is based on surveys covering the experiences of others. Such information is intended only as a general guide, to assist the family in reviewing its plan more objectively and to suggest alternatives that might enable the household to achieve its goals more effectively. A budget should be "workable," and this means that it should be simple, flexible, and designed to help each household achieve its objectives. Budgets may vary from household to household for several reasons—such as size of the family, style of living, health, taste, education, responsibilities, and other resources. Each budget should fit its family's unique combination of circumstances.

Records

Maintaining an elaborate record of weekly financial transactions in the home is bookkeeping and not budgeting. A detailed record of expenditures should be kept if this record of the family's spending patterns is needed to create the budget. However, after a pattern and guidelines for spending money are established, those persons responsible for establishing them should have little difficulty in remembering such information. They should not need to record every transaction made during the budgetary period. Of course, when checks are used, the amount and purpose should be recorded on the check stub or in the check register. Above all, the budget should not become a straitjacket in the sense that you are forbidden to deviate occasionally from the plan, regardless of new developments.

DEVELOPING THE BUDGET

The most likely starting point in budgeting is the family's weekly or monthly net income or take-home pay, that is, what is left after taxes and other payroll deductions. If you do not get the bulk of your income from wages and salaries, particular care should be taken in estimating the family's weekly or monthly income.

Many families make the mistake of including **contingent monetary receipts** as a part of their income for the household budget. In some cases, these contingent receipts are increased wages or bonuses that one of the family members expects but does not yet have. In other cases, the money expected is from the possible repayment of a loan from a debtor, or even from a gift. In numerous instances, families include expected refunds from income taxes as budget income for a specific month.

Families should keep records on the household's income and spending before drawing up a budget. These records should be kept for at least three months, using a form such as figure 3–1. Each family member must be diligent about reporting all cash purchases. The checkbook can be very helpful if care is taken to note on check

---

• **contingent monetary receipts:** money or income that an individual may or may not receive, depending on future developments.

Figure 3–1. Trial Run for Budget

INCOME	Jan.	Feb.	Mar.
Take-home pay	$		
Interest & dividends			
Total for month	$		

EXPENDITURES—Consumption	Jan.	Feb.	Mar.
Mortgage payment or rent	$		
Groceries			
Eating out			
Taxes			
Installment debt payment			
Fuel & utilities			
Transportation (auto expenses and bus fares)			
Medical care			
Clothing (purchases and care)			
Contributions to church and charities			
Special occasions (birthdays, celebrations, etc.)			
Miscellaneous (home repairs, dues to professional and social organizations)			
Savings			
TOTAL FOR MONTH	$		

stubs the purpose of every check written. Credit card bills can also be helpful. After a definite pattern for both income and spending is established, the pattern should be studied and then compared with the patterns of other families of similar size and circumstances. Such a comparison might prompt members of the family to review market information such as interest rates a bit more closely than before, and might persuade them to reexamine and to justify some of their previous expenditures. Then the family should establish a budget using a form similar to the one in figure 3–2.

SAVING A PLACE FOR SAVINGS

In addition to planning for routine expenditures, the family should make some provision for having money for unexpected or special obligations. These might include emergency expenditures, down payments on large purchases, expenses for repairs and maintenance on the home, and outlays designated for specific purposes, such as investments. One proven method of meeting these obligations is to

Figure 3–2. Monthly Budget

	MONTHLY BUDGETED AMOUNT	ACTUAL INCOME AND EXPENDITURES				MONTHLY TOTAL	DIFFERENCE BETWEEN BUDGET AND ACTUAL
		1st Week	2nd Week	3rd Week	4th Week		
INCOME							
Take-home pay							
Other income							
FIXED EXPENSES:							
Mortgage or rent							
Insurance—auto and other property							
Insurance—life							
Taxes							
Licenses, fees and dues							
Installment payments							
OPERATING EXPENSES							
Food							
Clothing							
Personal items							
Furnishings & equipment							
Utilities							
Auto and transportation							
Medical and dental							
Education							
Recreation							
Contributions							
Gifts and miscellany							
Discretionary personal funds							
Regular savings							
TOTALS							

include an item in the household budget for saving a specified amount from your weekly or monthly income, just as you set aside money for groceries, rent, or the electricity bill. Unfortunately, during the recent years of high inflation, many households spent more and more of their income to meet the rising cost of essentials. They did this without making a compensating reduction of spending for nonessentials such as vacations, recreation, and gifts. Members of these households have maintained their life styles, but they have also reduced or eliminated savings.

Households save for different reasons. Among the logical reasons are the following:

1. as a financial cushion for emergencies, such as serious illness, accidents, or prolonged unemployment;
2. for large recurring expenses, such as insurance premiums and various taxes;
3. for nonrecurring expenses, such as furniture and home improvements;
4. for short-term goals, such as vacations, Christmas gifts, and down payments toward the purchase of a home or car;
5. to take advantage of opportunities for business success or investment profit;
6. to supplement retirement pay and annuity payments.

Each household should decide why and how much it should save, independent of national averages and percentages suggested by various financial experts. Each household should save regularly, although there may be occasional circumstances or developments when the entire paycheck or income must be spent. On the other hand, there may be periods when the household's total income far exceeds its expenditures. During those periods, savings might be substantial.

INFORMAL METHODS OF BUDGETING

For those who are unable to maintain a formal budget, there are several procedures for evaluating and regulating household expenditures. All of these procedures are very informal and require very little time and effort. They include the following:

1. comparing the balance on the current monthly bank statement with the balance on previous statements;
2. comparing the total purchases on current credit card bills with total purchases on previous bills;
3. comparing the use of household cash during one period with use during similar periods in the past;
4. comparing current monthly bills for various utilities with previous bills.

None of these provides a detailed plan for allocating a family's income, or a means of following the expenditure pattern for every product and service used by the family. To some extent, however, if there is an increase in the level of expenditures, each of these alternatives can give a warning that something unusual is taking place in the family's finances, and that a detailed review of the family's expenditures is needed.

Balance on Bank Statements

Most people with accounts in banks or **thrifts** receive periodic statements that show deposits to each account, checks received for payment, the balance in the account at the beginning of the period, and the current balance. The date of the current balance usually coincides with the date of the statement itself. Unless the family's income has wide fluctuations, it is expected that the balance at the beginning of the period and the current balance will not vary significantly. When there is a wide variance, that is a signal for you and your family to review the expenditures as shown by the canceled checks. If the variance results from a scheduled payment that is unusually large, such as a quarterly, semiannual, or annual insurance premium, then there is no reason to suspect that the family is spending more on a particular item, e.g., entertainment, than is reasonable. If the change is unexpected and not due to a scheduled payment, then the family should discuss what the

---

• **thrifts:** a general term for savings and loan associations, credit unions, mutual savings banks, and savings banks.

household usually purchases during the period covered by the bank statement.

Aside from monitoring the difference between previous balances and current balances on the bank statement, you should be sensitive to a continuing decline or increase in your balance. A continuing decline obviously reflects a problem. More than likely, the family is spending more than it should. This should call for a serious review of the family's expenditures in order to reduce the expenditures on one or several items that the family usually purchases. On the other hand, a continuing increase indicates that more funds are kept in the checking account, sometimes called a **transactions account**, than are needed for current and **fixed expenses**.

If the money for quarterly, semiannual, and annual payments for particular items, such as taxes, is kept in your checking account, then a gradual increase in the balance of the transactions account is expected. On the other hand, if that money is kept in a separate account, then the steady rise in the current checking account balance means that more funds should be placed in investments that produce much higher yield than most simple checking accounts allow.

Credit Card Billings

With the increased use of credit cards to make purchases, consumers can now use the credit cards' billing statements to help monitor household spending. In fact, monthly credit card statements may be better for this than bank statements. Many stores now favor credit cards over personal checks. The consumer often finds it more convenient to use a credit card rather than a personal check when making a purchase. Credit cards are rarely, if ever, used to pay taxes or insurance premiums. These, however, are not usually the kind of discretionary expenditures that you might be spending too much money on.

- **transactions account:** any account on which checks are written regularly to pay bills.
- **fixed expenses:** expenses such as monthly rent or mortgage payments that must be paid at regular intervals, in set amounts, and do not vary with the activity in the household.

Your credit card bills show the date, vendor, and amount of the purchase, and the total amount of purchases for a specific period. Thus, if the totals begin to vary greatly from one month to another, you should review the bills, searching for the purchase responsible for the differences. The review may not reveal any expenditure that was unexpected. But it might show that the cost of certain items is more than what you normally spend on them.

Household Cash

Household cash is the money that should be available for food, gasoline, certain household supplies, allowances for the children, entertainment, and other items for which you usually pay cash. Certainly, the total amount of funds needed to serve these purposes is expected to vary from week to week or month to month, as there are different numbers of items to be purchased. If, however, the amount usually kept on hand for this purpose begins to fall short of the funds requested by members of the household, you should review the expenditures. Like the bank statement and the credit card bill, this type of monitoring of household cash requirements is not precise budgeting. However, if the household does not choose to use a formal budget, monitoring household cash can provide a means for determining whether family expenditures are staying within a normal pattern.

Utility Bills

Most families already compare utility bills for one period with those for previous periods. Utilities make up only a small part of household expenditures; nevertheless, the differences in such bills can provide a reason to review what is being spent for these items, and possibly a reason to review other expenditures as well. During particular periods, such as cold waves, the household may not want to adjust the use of certain utilities even if a review shows that the expenditures have been abnormally high. When this is the case, you and your family should take a closer look at other household expenditures with the idea of reducing them instead.

INFLATION AND THE CONSUMER PRICE INDEX

If our post–World War II experience can be used as a guide, then we are likely to face a persistent rise in the price of just about everything for many years to come. This general price rise is commonly known as **inflation**. Inflation usually results in shifts in the average family's household budget, because the family must still pay the rising costs of such basics as housing, utilities, transportation and medical care. For this and other reasons, you and your family should learn to measure the impact of inflation and constantly seek ways to minimize that impact on your economic well-being.

Compiling the CPI

One of the measures of inflation is the Consumer Price Index (CPI). The CPI is compiled by the U.S. Department of Labor and is designed to measure changes in the average price of a representative sample of goods and services purchased by urban consumers. Currently, the sample consists of some 400 items, often referred to as a "market basket," and includes food, housing, clothing, and transportation, among other things. The sample also includes items beyond the bare necessities, such as bowling fees, popular paperback books, textbooks, funeral services, and prenatal care. Here is how the CPI samples are weighed in the market basket:

Food accounts for 22.43 percent of the basket. So if food prices on the whole rise 10 percent, the overall CPI (if everything else stayed constant) would rise 2.243 percent. Food purchased in grocery stores is 17.89 percent of the index, while restaurant food is 4.54 percent.

Housing accounts for 33.23 percent of the market basket. That is broken down into rent, 5.5 percent; hotels 0.38 percent; cost of home ownership, such as mortgages and taxes, 14.27 percent; fuel oil and utilities, 5.26 percent; and household furnishings, such as appliances and operating expenses. 7.82 percent.

• **inflation:** a period of persistent rises in the general price level.

Clothing accounts for 10.63 percent.

Transportation makes up 13.88 percent, with the cost of automobiles 12.64 percent and public transportation the remaining 1.24 percent.

Health and recreation account for 19.45 percent.

Miscellaneous items cover the remaining 0.38 percent.

Announcements About the CPI

The CPI is announced each month by the federal government. The change is announced as a percentage increase or decrease from the previous month, and then this monthly figure is stated as if the same increase or decrease were to continue over twelve months. For example, the figure given in May might indicate that the change in the CPI for April was an 0.9 percent increase. In the same announcement, after **compounding**, the annual rate for this change would be given as an 11.6 percent increase.

Fitting the CPI to Your Situation

The CPI is the broadest measure of price changes affecting the consumer, although it does not necessarily represent a change in the cost of living for every individual. If a particular consumer buys more of the goods and services that are rising relatively fast, his or her cost of living will be rising faster than the CPI. Similarly, if another consumer's purchases are concentrated among the more stable items, his or her cost of living will rise more slowly than the CPI. Finally, if a family already owns its home, the "rental equivalent" portion of the housing component does not change from month to month, as it does for families who have adjustable-rate mortgages.

The CPI is not a comprehensive yardstick for the cost of living, as is often implied by the news media. The CPI, for example, does not measure the impact of personal income taxes at the federal, state,

---

• **compounding:** computing the new principal figure by using as a base both the previous principal and change accruing to that previous principal.

and local levels. Neither does it make allowances for substitutions in an individual's market basket as a counter to rising prices. When beef prices rise, a consumer may switch to chicken or fish, or something else that is less expensive. Some people might just eat less meat, using instead such items as beans, cheese, and other substitutes.

There are actually two official CPI's. One is known as the **CPI-W**, the cost of living index for urban wage earners and clerical workers. This is a revised version of the pre-1978 single CPI and the one that probably will continue to be used by labor negotiators. The other is known as the **CPI-U**, the all urban household index. This is the newest CPI and it covers about twice the number of consumers included in the CPI-W. In fact, the CPI-U reflects the buying of about eighty percent of the nation's total population. It includes people whose incomes are generally higher than average (self-employed, professional, white collar, and other salaried workers), plus those whose incomes tend to be lower (retired persons, others not in the labor force, and the unemployed).

While the CPI is not a perfect cost-of-living index, it is a reasonably good guide to the direction that consumer prices have been taking. If the index for the previous month indicates that prices rose seven percent, in all probability most consumers did pay more that month for their usual purchases.

IMPACT OF SPENDING ON BUDGETING

Notwithstanding the fact that consumers spend their incomes differently, and consequently are not affected in the same way by inflation, it is still useful to collect and review data on consumer spending to establish certain patterns of spending and to pinpoint periodic changes in these patterns. Organized data on consumer spending can serve as a guide to let you know how far your spending and saving vary from those of others in similar circumstances.

Understanding the interrelationship between budgeting and

- **CPI-W:** Consumer Price Index for Urban Wage Earners and Clerical Workers.
- **CPI-U:** Consumer Price Index for all Urban Consumers.

spending by the household is essential to financial progress. A budget is a plan for future spending, and such a plan is logically based on spending in the past. As a family's circumstances change, however, it is expected that adjustments will be made in the budget, and this, of course, means changes in the pattern of spending. The changing circumstances may be due to extended periods of high inflation, such as the American economy experienced from the mid-1970s until 1983, or the persistent loss in the **real income**, as was experienced by American consumers between 1985 and 1987.

When changing circumstances, such as rapid inflation and loss of real income, force the household to make signficant changes in its budget, and it appears that such changes are likely to result in a new pattern of expenditures, then it is time for the household to draw up a new budget. If frequent changes in planned spending are treated as temporary deviations from the budget, the family's life style is likely to remain unchanged. This, in turn, could mean creating more debt than the household's income can support. Once a family is in serious debt, seemingly the first budgetary item that is reduced or eliminated is savings. Reducing or eliminating savings could affect not only the long-term economic security of the household, but additions to current income as well.

Although circumstances beyond the family's control may necessitate new budgets from time to time, it is important to remember that, to be workable, your family's budget should be tailored for your family. It should be adapted to your family's needs and income, and it should always enjoy full cooperation from all members of the family. A budget is something you keep working and reworking until it "fits" your family and satisfies individual members. Sticking to a budget takes determination. However, if it is utilized as a spending plan, the end result will be more efficient spending and more value for the money spent.

• **real income:** an individual's income in dollars adjusted for a change in the price level.

4 ·
Tax
Planning

Although Mr. Curvey always knew the federal income provisions and paid all his taxes on time, he never planned his tax obligations, thus he always paid more taxes than he should have. For example, before the Tax Reform Act of 1986 was passed, all of Mr. Curvey's financial investments were in Treasury securities and certificates of deposits (CDs). Many of the yields on these investments were equal to or no better than the yields on some of the stocks that were available at the time. Thus, as a result of his lack of planning, Mr. Curvey always paid taxes on all of the income from his investment, instead of getting the $200 exclusion from gross income (he and his wife filed jointly) allowed for income from dividends.

After the passage of the Tax Reform Act of 1986, Mr. Curvey still failed to plan his family's tax obligations. He was aware that the deductibility of consumer debt–interest would be gradually phased out beginning with 1987 tax year, and he knew that he would need to borrow money to finance the purchase of a new car sometime during 1987. He had $12,000 in cash but decided to use these funds to buy long-term Treasury bonds yielding 8.5 percent. Auto dealers were offering to finance new cars at 6 percent for forty-eight months, and he thought that he would gain 2.5 percent by purchasing the Treasury bonds with his cash and borrowing to finance the car. He realized that only 65 percent of the interest on the automobile loan would be deductible in 1987 and that none of it would be deductible in 1991. He also knew that he could have borrowed $12,000 as a home equity loan and would have been able to deduct all of the interest, since his mortgage did not exceed the original cost of his house. He feared, however, that a home equity loan would jeopardize his family's security, and that he need not take that risk when he could borrow the money from the auto dealer and gain income from the Treasury bonds at the same time. With this as the scenario, one might ask, "Where was his lack of planning?"

Well, after giving more thought to the matter, Mr. Curvey would certainly have come up with another option. He could have carried through his plans to buy Treasury bonds with the $12,000, and he could have financed the car with a home equity loan and deducted all of the interest on the loan until it matured. What about jeopardizing the roof over his family's head? This would not have been a risk as long as he owned the $12,000 in Treasury bonds, because he could always sell these securities to repay the loan.

Thorough planning is essential for all taxpayers, and it can be crucial to the economic welfare of those taxpayers who hold investments and anticipate borrowing money. Because all taxpayers want to maximize their spendable income and minimize their tax liability, they should initiate their tax planning process by becoming reasonably familiar with current federal income tax provisions, along with any state and local income tax provisions. This does not mean that every taxpayer should seek to become a tax expert. It does mean, however, that each taxpayer has the responsibility of reading the information on taxes made available by the Internal Revenue Service (IRS), information published in the news media, and information in other sources, and utilizing this knowledge when making a decision to enter into a financial transaction.

While tax planning may be crucial to making investments and borrowing money, it should also play a role in making decisions in certain other matters. For example, if you have the option of renting an apartment or buying a home, you should review the effect that each of these options could have on your income tax liability before taking final action. Or, if you have the option of buying an expensive household appliance during the current year or postponing the purchase until the first part of the next year, a review of your tax alternatives should, again, play a role in your final decision.

In subsequent chapters on borrowing money, earnings on savings, buying stocks and bonds, purchasing government securities, and financing retirement, the importance and role of taxes will be discussed in detail. The remainder of this chapter will focus on the adjustments in planning that the average taxpayer should make in completing the transition from the era preceding the Tax Reform Act of 1986 to the present time, and will outline some of the practices, procedures, and courses of action that taxpayers should consider as a means of facilitating the tax planning process.

PRE–TAX REFORM ACT OF 1986 VS. THE PRESENT

When the Tax Reform Act of 1986 became effective as of the tax year beginning January 1, 1987, taxpayers should have considered some new elements in their tax planning. They should have recognized changes in the federal tax law that resulted in loss of the following tax "breaks":

1. extra personal exemption for taxpayers age sixty-five or older or blind (although to some extent this was replaced with a higher standard deduction);

2. personal exemption for a taxpayer (such as a child) who can be claimed as a dependent on another taxpayer's return;

3. the special $100 or $200 (filing jointly) dividend exclusion from gross income;

4. the 60 percent exclusion for long-term capital gains (100 percent of such gains are now subject to tax);

5. partial exclusion for unemployment benefits;

6. special deduction for married couples where both spouses work;

7. charitable deduction for non-itemizers (only itemizers are able to claim charitable deductions);

8. sales tax deduction for taxpayers who itemize;

9. partial credit for political contributions;

10. IRA deductions for certain taxpayers;

11. deductions for consumer interest (was phased out over a five-year period).

12. medical expenses (nondeductible portion was increased to 7.5 percent of **adjusted gross income [AGI]**).

• **adjusted gross income:** gross income (total income) minus any allowable adjustments to income.

13. moving expenses for non-itemizers;

14. most miscellaneous itemized deductions (including all un-reimbursed employee business expenses), which are now deductible only to the extent that they cumulatively exceed two percent of AGI;

15. the exclusion for scholarships and fellowships granted after August 16, 1986, that are not used for tuition and related expenses, or that are received by grantees who are not candidates for degrees;

16. the income averaging method of computing the tax;

17. the deduction for adoption expenses for children with special needs;

18. the installment method reporting certain income;

19. the reserve method for figuring bad debt deductions of taxpayers other than financial institutions.

In addition to planning for the new elements in the Tax Reform Act of 1986 that eliminated certain tax breaks, taxpayers should be planning for the new elements that resulted in *new* tax breaks. Those new breaks may be interpreted as follows:

1. increase in standard deductions for taxpayers who do not itemize;

2. increase in personal exemption;

3. increase in earned-income tax credit;

4. reduction in marginal tax rates, and the number of rates (there are now two rates: 15 percent and 28 percent);

5. elderly and blind taxpayers are entitled to an additional deduction of 600 if they are married and $750 if they are single.

SOURCES OF TAX INFORMATION

Before you embark upon any phase of your tax planning, you should make an effort to become familiar with the basic federal, state, and local income tax provisions. This book—more specifically this particular chapter—does not purport to be a source of tax information or a tax guide. For this kind of information, you should consult one or more of several popular publications—at least for information and guidance on federal income taxation. Most of these publications are priced very reasonably, and in fact, one is free. The following is a list of those that are easy to read, and that emphasize most of the information on taxation relevant to the average taxpayer:

• *Your Federal Income Tax.* The publisher is the IRS and you may obtain one free of charge from local offices of the IRS. You may also obtain a copy by calling a central telephone number at the IRS for "Free Tax Forms Only". When calling you should refer to this publication as publication 17.

• *The Arthur Young Tax Guide* (Ballantine). This document presents most, if not all, of what you will find in the IRS publication 17, plus discussions on tax planning and tax saving ideas.

• *J. K. Lasser's Your Income* (Simon and Schuster). This has been one of the more popular publications on federal income taxation for many years. It also has discussions on tax planning and crucial issues in the various tax provisions. One of the strengths of this publication is the numerous examples in which the tax provisions are applied to real-life situations.

• *Sylvia Porter's Income Tax Book* (Avon). This is a guide in which much of the information is presented in a question and answer form.

• *H & R Block Income Tax Workbook* (Collier). This is a very good tax guide for people who want to complete their own tax forms. It is well organized and contains tips on tax planning.

• *Pay Less Tax Legally* (Signet). This is a very useful tax guide written by a former IRS agent.

All of the aforementioned publications can be useful. However, for a thorough orientation on the federal income tax provisions, the free publication from the IRS may be your best source. The other publications may be better for tax planning and locating ways to reduce your tax liability. It may be advisable to browse through the table of contents and some of the inside discussions before you purchase any of the publications that are for sale.

THE PLANNING PROCESS

For the most part, the taxpayer's planning process simply calls for a reasonable knowledge of the various tax provisions, and the discipline needed to apply this knowledge to all the family's financial decisions. The following is a brief discussion of some decisions that many individuals are likely to face which will involve a tax provision in the Tax Reform Act of 1986, and for which some type of planning can reduce the individual's tax liability.

Joint or Separate Return

Before the Tax Reform Act of 1986, it was advisable for a married couple, with separate incomes taxed at two different rates, to file a joint return, because the average tax rate paid by the couple resulted in a tax saving. This decision is no longer crucial to the tax liability of the couple. Under current tax provisions, the ability to take some deductions is tied to an income threshold, which suggests that the averaging of the two incomes could mean that the spouse with the lower income would forego valuable tax savings. To achieve these savings in certain instances, however, would require planning at the beginning of the tax year.

To illustrate the advisability of the above suggestion, let us suppose one spouse has an AGI of $100,000 and the other spouse's AGI is $50,000. Further, suppose that the couple has miscellaneous expenses of $4,000. If they file jointly, they would be allowed to deduct only $1,000, which represents the amount in excess of 2 percent of the total AGI. If they plan at the beginning of the tax year for the lower salaried spouse to pay such miscellaneous expenses as fees paid to investment or brokerage firms for investment advice, the cost of renting the couple's safe-deposit box for storage of investment securities, and the fee for preparation of tax returns, and these amount to $4,000, then the deductible is $3,000, the amount in excess of 2 percent of $50,000 in AGI. This amounts to net tax saving of about $770.

Planning for filing a joint return or separate returns could also reduce the tax liability of a married couple as a result of the current tax provision on the Individual Retirement Account (IRA). Let us assume that one of the spouses is covered by an employer pension plan, and that the couple filed a joint return before the Tax Reform Act of 1986. Under current tax law, the deductibility of an IRA contribution begins to be phased out for both spouses when the total AGI exceeds $40,000. Filing separately, however, the spouse with an employer that has a pension plan may fall below income restrictions, while the spouse without a qualified retirement plan will be able to deduct IRA contributions.

Children's Income (Under fourteen years old)

Before the Tax Reform Act of 1986, many taxpaying parents were able to reduce their taxes on income that they planned for their children to receive. This was done by establishing the so-called Clifford trusts, in which the child would receive income from assets placed in a trust for, say, ten years, and after that period, the assets would revert back to the parent. In the meantime, the parents would have avoided the taxes on that income. Under current tax provisions, this strategy is now useless, because a child's net unearned income may be subject to tax at the parent's tax rate if the child has not reached age fourteen at the close of the tax year and either parent is alive at the close of that year. The net unearned income is the child's unearned income, such as interest, dividends, and royalties in excess of $500, plus the greater of either $500 or the child's itemized deductions that are directly connected with the production of the unearned income.

With the proper planning, parents of children under age fourteen can still achieve part of the objectives sought under the old Clifford trusts. In general, these parents can start buying securities or other investments that defer the income—or a significant part of it—until the child reaches age fourteen. These securities could include **zero-coupon bonds** and non-dividend–paying growth stocks. Investments could include a mutual fund that invests in non-dividend–paying growth stocks. With this particular investment, not only are

---

• **zero coupon bond:** a bond that pays no interest. It is sold at a deep discount at time of issuance; and thus the buyer's gain is the difference between the discount price and face value of the bond collected at maturity.

there no dividends to tax, but any capital gains can be taken after the child reaches age fourteen and is no longer taxed at the parents' presumably higher rate.

Borrowing Money

For many years, individuals have borrowed money either directly or indirectly to purchase such items as household appliances, household furnishings, automobiles, and even clothing. Furthermore, individuals have been able to deduct the interest on this borrowed money in filing their federal income tax. Prior to the Tax Reform Act of 1986, the deductibility of all personal interest was a definite—if not crucial—factor in the planning of many purchases by taxpayers, because this deductibility actually meant that the federal government was paying a portion of the interest on the borrowed money. Thus, when the maximum tax rate was 50 percent, before the passage of the Tax Reform Act, many taxpayers when faced with, say, $300 in interest charges on a purchase made on credit, would respond by saying, "Well, since Uncle Sam will pay half of this $300, I see no problem with borrowing the money to buy this item."

The story is very different under current tax provisions, in which the amount of personal interest expense allowed as an itemized deduction on Schedule A, Form 1040 is generally limited to only a portion of the interest that the individual pays. Except for a limited amount of mortgage interest as discussed below, after 1990 no deduction will be allowed for personal interest paid or accrued during the year. Personal interest generally includes interest paid on car loans, credit cards, installment loans, and personal loans.

The percentage of personal interest that you may now deduct, beginning in 1987 and through 1990, is as follows:

Tax Year Beginning	Deductible Percentage
1987	65%
1988	40
1989	20
1990	10

For the tax years beginning after December 31, 1986, the interest that you incur on a mortgage or a line of credit secured by your principal residence or second residence is generally deductible only to the extent that the total amount of debt secured by the residence is not more than the lower of either: the fair market value of the residence, OR the cost (basis) of the residence, plus the cost of home improvements, plus the amount of debt incurred after August 16, 1986 for qualified educational expenses.

For mortgages secured by the residence prior to August 17, 1986, interest is deductible only to the extent that the mortgage does not exceed the fair market value of the residence. This rule applies regardless of how the borrowed funds are used.

How can you plan for the deductibility of personal interest under the current tax law? In the first place, you can consider borrowing against the equity in your home to pay for any purchases that you customarily buy or credit, or on installment, or with funds from a personal loan. As long as you don't borrow any more than the original cost of your home plus the cost of *improvements*, the interest is fully deductible, no matter how you use the money. However, if you borrow against the *appreciated* value of your home, only the interest on the funds that you use for medical and educational purposes is deductible.

Beginning in the 1987 tax year, persons who refinance their homes, obtain second mortgages or borrow against the equity in their home, by way of a home equity loan, will have to file the new IRS Form 8598.

In calculating the amount of equity in a home that may be used for collateral on a home mortgage loan, you may confront a problem in trying to identify the cost of your home improvements. There are no questions about outlays for such things as an added room, a fence, or even the installing of new plumbing or wiring. But what about replacement of a tile floor with one that is sanded with the underlying wood coated with polyurethane? Also, what about a repair that results in something clearly better than the original? One guide for planning is that a genuine home improvement is a change that increases the value of your home and will help to extend its life. From this point, you can seek sometimes to turn a "repair" into an "improvement." This can be accomplished by permitting needed repairs to accumulate and then have them all done as part of an extensive remodeling or restoration of your home. If you plan to try this approach, you should be prepared to support your claims with invoices and copies of contracts. If you retain the canceled checks to go along with these documents, your case will be that much stronger.

INVESTMENTS

As indicated earlier, taxpayers are no longer allowed a dividend exclusion. Prior to the Tax Reform Act of 1986, you could exclude up to $100 of total qualifying dividends (or up to $200 on a joint return). This change could bring about an adjustment in planning your future portfolio.

Before the passage of the Tax Reform Act, you may have purchased stocks with potential growth but with a low payout of dividend. You may have been willing to accept the low payout because you knew that up to $100 ($200 on a joint return) would not be taxed at all. All of the cash dividend would enter your family's cash flow. At the same time, you knew that if the funds used for the purchase of this stock were used instead to purchase a bank CD, the interest earnings could be taxed up to 50 percent—depending, of course, on your specific marginal tax rate.

Under current tax provisions, however, your planning might suggest that you forego investment in stocks with a low payout of dividends, and concentrate more on, say, Treasury notes and bonds, or bank CDs. These securities would provide you with relatively more cash than the stocks with the low payout of dividends, and relatively more cash than before because of the lower marginal tax rates under the current tax law.

Investment Interest Deduction

Like the deduction for personal or consumer interest, the deductibility of interest on loans connected with your investments is different than it was before the Tax Reform Act of 1986. Prior to this change in the tax law, you were allowed a deduction of interest of up to the amount of your net investment income, plus up to $10,000 ($5,000 if you were married and filing separately) of investment interest in excess of your net investment income. Beginning with the 1987 tax year, the excess interest amount was phased out. For 1987, you were allowed a deduction of up to the amount of your net investment income plus 65 percent of any excess, but not more than $6,500 ($3,250 for persons filing separately). For the tax years 1988, 1989, and 1990, the deductible percentages are the same as those that apply to the phase-out of the personal interest deduction— namely 40, 20, and 10 percent respectively.

In planning for this change in the deductibility of investment interest, you may, of course, borrow the funds against the equity in you home, in much the same way as you would borrow to purchase consumer items. In both instances, the interest would be deductible. However, in the case of borrowing funds for purposes of investment, you should remember that even under the new tax law, the interest is deductible regardless of the source of the borrowed funds. The limitation on this deductibility applies only to interest in excess of the net investment income.

Investment interest includes interest paid or accrued on money you borrow to buy or carry property held for investment. In determining your investment interest, you should not include any amounts that you accounted for in determining your income or loss from a **passive activity**. Likewise, do not include interest expense that is allocable to a rental real property activity in which you actively participated (this falls within the definition of the passive loss rule).

Unlike the deduction of personal interest, the amount of investment interest that you cannot deduct under current tax provisions can be carried forward to the next tax year, and may then be deducted to the extent that you have net investment income that exceeds your investment interest in that later year. However, any carryover may not be used in determining any excess interest in that later year.

Any planning for the deductibility of interest on funds used for an investment should always consider the interest as one of the costs associated with making the investment. Thus, in planning to make

---

• **passive activity:** any activity that involves the conduct of any trade or business, and in which the taxpayer does not materially participate. Any rental activity is considered a passive activity even if the taxpayer does materially participate in the activity.

additional investments that would involve additional costs, such as interest on borrowed money, you should apply the well-known economic principle known as marginal analysis. That is, you should try to make certain that any investment decision will add at least as much to your investment income as it does to your investment costs. While this does not have to be the sole factor in your investment decision, it will ensure that you will not lose any ground on the relationship between your income on an investment and the interest cost associated with your investments.

Capital Gains and Losses

The 60 percent long-term capital gains deduction was repealed effective January 1, 1987. Thus, under current tax provisions, you must treat all capital gains, whether short-term or long-term, as ordinary income. This repeal, however, does not affect the rule that allows you to postpone the gain on the sale or exchange of your principal residence, if you purchase another principal residence with a purchase price that is at least as much as the adjusted basis of the residence sold. In addition, the repeal does not affect the rule that allows you a one-time exclusion of $125,000 of gain on the sale of your principal residence if you are fifty-five years of age or older.

Capital losses will be allowed in full against capital gains, plus up to $3,000 of ordinary income. The excess of net long-term capital loss over net short-term capital gain will be allowed in full. You no longer have to reduce long-term capital losses by 50 percent before applying them against ordinary income. You may still carry forward to future years those capital losses not fully deductible in the current tax year.

The loss of the generous deduction for long-term capital gains under the Tax Reform Act of 1986 simply means that taxpayers should give more consideration to investments that produce income, as opposed to those that promise capital appreciation. Also, because there is no longer a distinction between long-term and short-term capital gains, you have no incentive to defer selling a recently purchased stock or other asset in order to cross the six-month threshold and gain the long-term benefit.

All investments involve some risk. Under current tax provisions, however, you will no longer be compensated by the federal government through the prospect of a deduction for making a relatively high-risk investment. Counting on long-term gains is taking a risk that is higher than usual. In planning your investment portfolio, then, you are virtually compelled to buy less risky investments and to favor those investments that are producing income today, as opposed to those that promise to produce income tomorrow.

YOUR TAX RATES

Throughout the planning for your tax liability, you should always be conscious of your marginal tax rate. Your specific marginal tax rate is the rate at which the last dollar of your income is taxed. For 1988 and beyond, only two marginal tax rates will be levied: 15 percent and 28 percent. The table below shows how these two rates are imposed on your taxable income:

Tax Rate	Single	Married Filing Jointly and Qualfying Widow(er)
15%	$0–$17,850	$0–$29,750
28%	over $17,850	over $29,750

Tax Rate	Married Filing Separately	Head of Household
15%	$0–$14,875	$0–$23,900
28%	over $14,875	over $23,900

For tax years beginning after 1988, the amount of taxable income in each bracket will be adjusted, if necessary, so that taxes will not increase due to inflation.

Beginning in 1988, the benefit of the 15 percent bracket is phased out for taxpayers having taxable income exceeding certain dollar amounts. Taxable income above the applicable dollar amounts will be subject to an additional 5 percent tax (subject to limitations). The applicable dollar amounts of taxable income above which the additional tax will apply are shown in the following table:

Filing Status	Applicable Dollar Amount
Single	$43,150
Married Filing Jointly and Qualifying Widow(er)	71,900
Married Filing Separately	35,950
Head of Household	61,650

The applicable dollar amounts will be adjusted for inflation, if necessary, beginning in 1989.

RECORD-KEEPING

It goes without saying that maintaining good records of financial transactions is an indispensable component of tax planning. In fact, some aspects of tax planning are dependent upon taxpayers' records of previous financial transactions.

While you probably have a limited amount of space in your home that you can devote to maintaining financial records, it is essential that you find the space necessary for storing and maintaining those records that could result in significant tax savings or severe tax penalties at some future time. In general, you should maintain records of all financial transactions that you feel might have a bearing on your tax obligations and tax decisions. This means that you should demand and save all receipts, cancelled checks, invoices, statements of accounts, and other evidence to prove that certain transactions have taken place and that certain funds have been expended by you in connection with such transactions. These documents should be kept as long as they are important for any tax law.

Records that support an item of income or a deduction appearing on your federal tax return should be kept until the **statute of limitations** for the tax return runs out. Usually, this is three years from the date the tax return was due or filed, or two years from the date the federal tax was paid, whichever is later. Sometimes,

---

• **statute of limitations:** a law that bars suits upon valid claims after a specified period of time.

however, it may be advisable to keep records for a longer period. For example, records relating to the purchase of your home should be kept as long as they are needed to compute the basis of the original or replacement property. Certainly, you should keep copies of previous tax returns for more than three years, because it is always possible that new tax laws will give tax benefits to taxpayers who can prove by their records from previous years that they are entitled to such benefits. Above all, you should keep on file any and all correspondence with the IRS.

5 ·

Making Money On Borrowed Money

Many people are reluctant to borrow money. There are even a few who refuse to borrow when it is the only way they can buy a necessity such as a home, car, large appliance, or furniture. Reasons for this reluctance to borrow money are varied. In some cases, it is a matter of principle. Some people take the attitude, "If I don't have the money to pay for it, I can't afford it. And if I can't afford it, I'll just do without it until I can afford it. I just don't like debt hanging over my head." Others don't like the risk involved when borrowing money. They fear they may lose their down payment or their **collateral**, thereby winding up in a worse predicament than they were in before they borrowed the money. Then, of course, there are those who dislike borrowing money because they don't like the idea of paying interest. They regard lenders who charge interest as parasites, because the lenders, in their opinion, "don't do anything to earn the money paid out in interest." People in this group become upset when they review the following data on a thirty-year mortgage loan:

1. A homeowner would pay $118,120 to borrow $32,000 at 15 percent interest.

• **collateral:** something of value pledged to assure repayment of a loan and subject to seizure if the loan is not repaid.

2. A homeowner would pay $130,640 to borrow $40,000 at 14 percent interest.

3. A homeowner would pay $140,600 to borrow $52,000 at 12 percent interest.

While those statistics may be a bit disconcerting at first glance, we must realize that interest is a price paid for the use of something that is very valuable—namely, other people's money—and that the borrowed money provides significant value to the borrower at the time of the loan. Most families understand this principle and are willing to borrow when the resultant value is the enjoyment of such things as a home, car, appliance, or furniture. They are unsure, however, about borrowing when the resultant value is something less tangible, such as an investment in securities, which could produce additional income for the family.

TAX DEDUCTION FOR INVESTMENT INTEREST

Borrowing money for the purpose of making money is often referred to as a form of **leveraging**, and despite the change in the Tax Reform Act of 1986, those borrowing for this purpose still receive assistance from Uncle Sam. As indicated in the chapter on "Tax Planning," you can deduct interest on loans for investment to the extent that you have net investment income. The amount of interest that you cannot deduct can be carried forward to the next year and can be deducted to the extent that you have net investment income that exceeds your investment interest in that later year.

WHEN TO BORROW

There are situations in which you can make money by borrowing money, and such situations need not be unrealistic. In most cases, you need only a modest amount of savings and some basic

---

• **leveraging:** the act of buying income-producing assets (such as stocks, bonds, or real estate) with a relatively modest amount of the buyer's own funds and a significant amount of funds from other sources.

information about investment opportunities—the kind of information found in the local newspaper. Let's look at two situations and see how close they come to your potential for making money on borrowed money.

Situation 1.   Let's assume that you know about an upcoming offer of four-year Treasury notes that are likely to earn 9 percent interest. The **minimum denomination** of these notes is $1,000. Let's also assume that you have only $500 in a passbook savings account earning 4 percent, but that you also have a life insurance policy with a cash value of $500. This policy has a **loan provision** that allows you to borrow the cash value at an interest rate of 5 percent. The loan and subsequent purchase of a $1,000 Treasury note will result in the following:

> Interest earnings on the Treasury note
>   for the year $90.00
> Interest earnings foregone
>   on your passbook savings account. . . . . ($20.00)
> Interest paid on the policy loan . . . . (25.00)
>   (45.00)
> Net gain for the year $45.00

There are other additions to this potential net gain. One of these would be the exemption of the $90 in interest earnings from any state and local income tax. Interest earnings on Treasury securities, however, are subject to federal income taxes. Another gain would be the deduction on your federal income tax of the $25 in interest paid on the policy loan.

Situation 2.   In this situation, let's assume that you have used personal money management strategies for several years, and have now accumulated investments in CDs and Treasury bills that total

- **minimum denomination:** smallest amount you can buy.
- **loan provision:** a clause in the policy that explains how the policyholder can borrow up to the total accumulated cash value of the policy.

$50,000 and are currently yielding an average of 7 percent. Let's also assume that these investment instruments will mature within the next week, and that you plan to invest the entire $50,000 in five-year Treasury notes. You have noted that these notes are currently yielding 9 percent.

On August 15, the day of the auction of these Treasury bonds, you submit your check for $50,000 to the Federal Reserve Bank. On the next day you learn that both the yield and the **coupon interest rate** on the notes are 8 percent, and three days after the auction, the Federal Reserve Bank sends you a letter requesting an additional $1,000. You call the Federal Reserve Bank and you are told that this additional amount is to cover the accumulated interest on these notes from May 15, the date of the last scheduled interest payment, to August 15, the effective date of purchase of the notes. This procedure is to accommodate the U.S. Treasury's system of making only two interest payments a year. On November 15, you will receive a direct deposit to your bank account for a full six-months' interest in the amount of $2,000; however, you still have the problem of raising an additional $1,000.

This is another situation in which you can make money by borrowing money. As a regular customer of a bank, you should be able to take out a **signature loan** for the $1,000 needed to complete the purchase of the Treasury notes. Even if you are charged a rate of 11 percent, the interest of a ninety-day loan would amount to only $27.50. In ninety days, or on November 15, you would receive an interest check for $2,000. This would enable you to pay off the loan and still have a sizable return on your investment. Your net gain would be as follows:

Earnings on Treasury bond for ninety days............$1,000.00
Interest charged on $1,750 for ninety days...............(27.50)
      Net gain on transaction ....$ 972.50

* **coupon interest rate:** the interest rate specified on the bond certificate and on the interest coupons attached to a bond certificate.
* **signature loan:** a loan granted on the basis of a borrower's credit worthiness and signature; not secured by collateral.

This net gain of $972.50 would exceed the three months' interest of $875 that would have been earned on the $50,000 had it been reinvested in the previously held securities. This would hold true even if the yield on these previously held securities had increased. Experience shows that the yield on intermediate-term (four to seven year) Treasury securities always exceeds the yield on bank CDs and Treasury bills.

In situation one, you might conclude that the net gain from the transactions involved borrowed money was rather small. This may be true in view of the prices that a person must pay today for various goods and services. However, the net gain increases with the amount of money you invest in the various options, a factor that suggests the possibility of greater gains when greater amounts of resources are available.

Another factor to consider when viewing the size of the net gain from investing borrowed money is the saying, "You've got to crawl before you can walk." The implication is that if you are a neophyte in this type of financial exercise, you should be content initially to experiment with small amounts of money. In the event that something goes wrong, the loss will be small.

SOURCES OF LOANS

When your objective is to make a profit from or finance your investments with borrowed money, you should scrutinize all of the sources of borrowed money. By finding the source with the lowest net cost of borrowing, you can maximize your profit. When the collateral consists of CDs, your sources for a loan may be restricted to the depository institution that issued the CD. This is not to say that other lenders will refuse CDs from other institutions as collateral, but securing the loan from the issuing institution will be easier. In general, the most convenient source for borrowing money is the lending institution with which you have some type of financial relationship. The following are five common sources for loans to finance your investments.

MARGIN LOANS

Margin loans are made when the investor borrows money from his or her broker to help finance the purchase of securities. This method of buying securities will be discussed in more detail in the chapter on "Stocks and the Stock Market."

If you would like to make money by borrowing money, you may want to consider doubling the amount of securities you can buy with your present cash resources by borrowing an equal amount of money from your broker. The interest paid on such borrowed funds is deductible when filing federal income tax returns, up to the extent of your net investment income from interest, dividends, and capital gains. For interest in excess of this net income, 40 percent will be deductible in 1988, 20 percent will be deductible in 1989, and 10 percent will be deductible in 1990. After 1990, excess interest will not be deductible. However, any disallowed part of your interest cost can be carried forward indefinitely to offset net investment income.

When an investor takes a loan from a broker to buy stock, the amount of the loan is restricted by the margin requirements set by the Federal Reserve system. Currently, the requirement is 50 percent. This means that the maximum loan on the purchase of stock from a broker cannot exceed 50 percent of the price of the stock. To open a margin account, the investor signs an agreement with the broker that gives use of the stock and some control over the account to the broker. The stock serves as collateral for the loan. Should the amount of collateral in the account fall below a specified level, the broker can require that the investor put more assets in the account. This is referred to as a **margin call**, and the investor can send the broker either more cash or more securities as collateral. If the investor fails to meet a margin call, then the broker will sell some of the securities in the account to supply the cash needed to protect the loan.

• **margin call:** a demand from a broker to repay part of a loan used to help purchase stock, if the value of the stock falls below a certain percentage of the outstanding loan amount.

If a person borrows abroad, he must comply with the margin regulation as if the credit were obtained in the United States—even if the foreign lender is not subject to any margin regulation.

A borrower is subject to prosecution if a violation of the law or regulation is willful. Any person who willfully aids or abets the violation of any provision of Federal Reserve regulations is considered to be a violator and can be prosecuted.

Buying on margin can provide you with a means to increase leverage, and therefore maximize the return on your investment. However, a decline in value of securities purchased on margin could cause you to suffer severe losses. It is not unusual for an entire margin account to be liquidated at a substantial loss because the securities in the account declined in value. Therefore, you must carefully and continually monitor the value of securities purchased on margin.

INSURANCE POLICY LOANS

If you have a life insurance policy, a cash value accumulates as long as you maintain the policy. The policy shows the cash value that accumulates each year. Each policy has a provision for borrowing the cash value, including the rate of interest to be charged on the loan. Depending on when the policy was purchased, the rate could range from 5 to 8 percent.

In most cases, the insurance company bills the policyholder for the annual interest. If the interest is not paid, the company will add the interest to the loan. If the policyholder pays the interest, then that interest is tax-deductible in accordance with the Tax Reform Act of 1986.

If the loan on the policy is not paid, the **proceeds of the policy** will be reduced by the amount of the loan. This, of course, reduces the payout to the policyholder's beneficiaries.

There is really little need to pay off a loan on a policy. The reduced payout to the beneficiary can be made up by investing the

---

* **proceeds of the policy:** the total amount of the insurance policy realized or to be received by the beneficiary when the policy is paid off.

borrowed funds in the beneficiary's name or in a joint survivorship account in your name and the beneficiary's name. The interest earnings can be used at your discretion.

LOANS AGAINST SAVINGS DEPOSITS

Another source of funds to finance your investments is a loan secured by your savings account or certificate of deposit. Many banks and savings and loan associations offer such loans at 2 to 3 percent above the rate that they are paying on your money. You continue to earn interest on your savings, but you cannot make withdrawals as long as the loan is outstanding. In most cases, the lending institutions will limit the amount of your loan to a maximum of 80 percent of the face value of your savings instruments.

CREDIT UNIONS

Credit unions often offer good value in personal loans. They often require less stringent qualifications and provide faster service on loans than do banks or thrifts. In many cases, their loans are cheaper and their savings rates more attractive. And while consumer lending is still their bread-and-butter business, some of the larger unions have recently been offering financial services such as credit cards, individual retirement accounts, discount brokerage services, automated teller machine networks, and computer-authorized loans.

Most credit unions are connected to corporations. But the number serving a company varies, since employees in different units or plants of the same firm may decide to set up their own. International Business Machines Corporation, for example, has twenty, while Bechtel Group Inc. has one. The extent of corporate involvement also differs. Some companies agree only to deduct loan payments and savings installments from members' paychecks and apply them to credit union accounts. Others, like Hewlett-Packard Co., also provide staff and office space. Regardless of the extent of involvement, credit unions are prohibited from releasing members' financial information to companies.

Joining a credit union is simple. Membership fees, if any, are nominal, as is the paperwork. Some credit unions require members to be enrolled for three to six months before they can take out loans, but others allow borrowing on the first day. Also, many credit unions extend membership privileges to the immediate family, and, in some cases, to other relatives or even unrelated housemates.

Each credit union sets its own loan criteria, and unions are generally easier to borrow from than banks because they require less customer information. Also, the amounts that can be borrowed, even unsecured, tend to be substantial.

On the other hand, even though financial services are expanding at larger unions, most don't provide first mortgages, and virtually all are prevented from holding trust accounts or making commercial loans.

COMMERCIAL BANKS

Most banks will make signature loans of up to $2,500, which should be sufficient to cover the kinds of investments that you would want to consider. Of course, banks will also make personal loans where there is proper collateral.

When considering a bank as a source for a personal loan, you should not be encouraged to borrow more than you actually need because the so-called prime rate reported by newspapers appears to be reasonable or perhaps even falling. This is supposedly the interest rate that banks charge their best customers, but it is most often applied to corporate best customers, particularly those that borrow for short periods of time. Personal loans are often for longer periods and the rates of interest charged on these loans usually exceed the prime rate.

There are other sources from which you can borrow money to make investments. Among these are finance companies, brokers, and various dealers. However, the cost of loans from these sources is likely to exceed even the highest cost loans from insurance companies and savings institutions. Currently, a policy loan is by far the lowest cost loan that you can obtain. When this source is exhausted, you should shop among the other sources to find the next best deal.

NEGOTIATING A LOAN

Before discussing how to negotiate a loan, perhaps we should discuss briefly the matter of how to establish yourself for borrowing. First, you should maintain a checking or savings account (or combination of the two) at a local bank or savings institution. This will establish your financial identity and give you access to several services and privileges, including personal loans. As a second step, many credit and consumer counselors suggest that you apply for a small personal loan secured by your savings. You are urged to pay off this loan as scheduled, thereby establishing a good credit history and qualifying for larger loans if needed.

After establishing a good credit history, you are ready for the mechanics of borrowing. The first step is to have a clear purpose for burrowing the money and the ability to explain this purpose to the lending officer, along with a knowledge of the specific amount of money you wish to borrow.

During your negotiation of the loan with the lending officer, you will need one document from home, namely, an updated net worth statement as described in chapter 2. As you will recall, this statement lists all of the items that you use and own in the household, and all of your debts. In case you are applying for a signature loan, the lending officer would want to review your current debts or liabilities. If the loan is one in which collateral is required, the lending officer would want to examine your assets for suitable collateral. To have your financial assets considered for collateral, you should attach a sheet providing key information—such as date of purchase, **face value**, rate of interest, issuing source, and owners of record—on each financial instrument. You may also want to attach a supplemental statement on your liabilities or debts. The lending officer will want to know the source and nature of the debts and the amount and frequency of payments. Such information

---

• **face value:** for insurance, face value is the dollar value that expresses coverage limits; it appears on the front of the policy. For a bond, face value refers to the money amount for which the bond can be redeemed at maturity. It is not an indication of market value.

as your current employer, income, and rate of savings can be given verbally. This last item is important because it can convince the lending officer of your ability to pay off a loan despite any problems with the expected return from the investment.

If the loan is granted, make sure that you have a clear understanding of all aspects of the loan. This includes the effective rate of interest, the repayment schedule, the penalty for late payment, and the collateral, if any, that is required.

FINAL JUDGEMENT

Fortunately, if you are inclined to make or earn money with borrowed money, Uncle Sam will still assist you in achieving your objective. Although current federal income tax provisions in this area are not quite as generous as those of the pre–Tax Reform Act of 1986 era, the deduction for interest on funds borrowed for investment can still be crucial to building your portfolio.

In the final analysis, the questions of when, where, and how to borrow money for the purpose of investing will depend upon your individual circumstances, the nature of the prospective investment, and your analysis of the prospective gain from the loan. A loan of the cash value from your life insurance policy is by far the most advantageous of the various sources of loans. The interest rate on this loan is the lowest, the procedure for borrowing is the simplest, the paperwork involved is far less than the other sources, and the loan requirements are the least complicated. For just these reasons, however, you can be tempted to put this money in investments without making the proper analysis beforehand. Such temptations should be avoided. Making a profit on borrowed money is a hallmark of personal money management. The manager must make certain, however, to observe all of the rules suggested in the training for personal money management.

6 ·

Extra Earnings From Savings

It is frequently said that the three biggest lies are: "The check is in the mail," "I'll do it tomorrow," and "You'll have the car back by noon." Although these certainly qualify as the most frequently heard, there is one more that's a candidate for that list: "We don't earn enough money to think about savings."

Experience shows that there is no such thing as having too little income to have a savings program. The limitation among households with modest incomes is knowledge, not income. An understanding of personal money management can convince the members of these households of the value of setting up a systematic savings program, and can show them how to start one with little effort. Sound personal money management indicates that savings should be treated as just another expenditure. A certain amount should be taken from a household's take-home pay each pay period and placed in a passbook savings account in much the same way you would pay the rent or the mortgage payment.

In setting up a savings program, you should initially save to satisfy basic needs and desires. You should, for example, save to have a financial cushion for emergencies (serious illness, accidents, or prolonged unemployment); to meet large recurring expenses (insurance premiums and various tax payments); to finance vacations and buy Christmas gifts; and to accumulate down payments for future purchases, such as furniture, a car, or a home.

After making sure that you have enough money in your passbook account to take care of emergencies and certain designated future expenditures, you should consider earning money on your addition-al savings. At this point in your financial program, your additional money should still be considered as savings and not funds available for investment. With investments, there is no definite guarantee of the return of the amount invested, or the interest earnings on the investment. Also, upon liquidating investments, you could receive less money than you originally put in. The safety of invested money depends solely upon the safety of the investment instrument. Investments entail the kind of risk that should not be taken by a household with a limited income or a limited amount of funds at its disposal. The cutoff point for "limited income" or "limited amount of funds at its disposal" is not a precise figure in terms of dollars and cents. A reasonable guideline, however, may take the form of the impact that the possible loss of the funds will have on the overall standard of living for the household. If the loss of these funds will have a significant impact on what the household will or will not spend for its total income, then the funds should still be considered as savings.

It is important to use your money to make more money, even if the amount you're able to save is modest. If you're a small saver, saving to make money should be one of your purposes for saving, but avoid the temptation of seeking quick and high profits on your savings. Of course, high risks sometimes bring high profits, but if you're a small saver, avoid the higher risks because of your limited resources. When households with modest incomes forego buying some of the luxuries of life to accumulate savings, a loss of such savings through high-risk ventures can discourage future attempts to save, and in the long run deprive the household of a higher standard of living.

Whether you're saving to meet basic needs and desires or saving to make a profit, it is essential to have a savings plan. There are various financial arrangements that may be best suited for helping your savings grow into even bigger savings.

SAVINGS PLAN

If you and the members of your household feel that you have no savings because you're unable to find any money to save, you need to find money to save. In chapter 3, one of the suggestions made for practical budgeting was to closely monitor the balance in your monthly banking statement. It was suggested that a steadily decreasing balance should serve as a red flag, indicating that you needed to review your monthly expenditures. If the balance showed a steady increase, you might have had surplus funds that were not earning any interest or were earning much less interest than they should.

If your bank balance has been decreasing steadily, it is logical to assume that saving will be difficult. The decreasing bank balance is a problem itself, and to keep it from becoming a steadily worsening one, review all of your expenditures. After the review, you will be compelled to eliminate or reduce the amount of certain expenditures. During this exercise, take a second look at some of these expenditures and find sufficient reductions to not only stop the pattern of a declining bank balance, but also raise extra funds that can immediately be earmarked for savings. Just think, what would you do if gasoline prices were to increase from $1.00 a gallon to $1.50 a gallon? If you are truthful, the answer is that you would reduce or cut out something else in order to pay the additional $.50 a gallon. It is this $.50 multiplied by the number of gallons of gasoline that you normally use during a week or month that can be used to start and maintain a savings program. The same kind of reasoning can be applied if the price of gasoline has dropped from $1.50 to $1.00 a gallon during the past several weeks. What happens to this extra $.50 multiplied by X number of gallons? This kind of thinking is a realistic answer for those who believe that they do not earn enough money to save regularly.

On the other hand, if your bank balance has been steadily increasing each month, it is obvious that you have surplus funds for a savings program. You should then settle on a bank balance that approximates what you feel is adequate for your financial transactions each month, and proceed to transfer the rest each month to a **savings instrument** as a part of your systematic savings plan. Knowing that your balance is running a surplus each month, you

---

* **savings instrument:** any contractual agreement with a financial institution in which the saver is assured of interest earnings on his or her funds.

might be tempted to deposit less each month into this checking or transactions account and deposit more into some type of savings account. This is fine, as long as you are certain that there will be no extraordinarily large expenditures that month. Above all, make sure that your balance will cover your checks at all times. Thus, to ensure safety, you may favor letting the surplus accumulate first, then remove it as a part of your savings plan. At any rate, you should make every effort to identify a surplus in your monthly balance as soon as possible, and then take steps to convert this surplus to savings.

FEDERAL INSURANCE FOR SAVERS

Regardless of where you keep your savings, it is important that they are kept safe. One safe place, for example, is any financial depository institution where the funds are insured by an agency of the U.S. government. Funds in these institutions are insured up to $100,000 per depositor. Using these institutions, a small family can have a sizeable total of savings, all insured, by setting up properly prepared individual, joint, and trust accounts. In fact, figure 6–1 shows that it is possible for a family consisting of only a husband and wife to have federal insurance coverage for savings of up to $500,000. How do you get this federal insurance? Simply deposit your savings in a financial institution that displays prominently on its premises one of the following official signs:

1. FDIC: This sign represents the Federal Deposit Insurance Corporation, which is an agency of the federal government that insures accounts at commercial banks, savings banks, and mutual savings banks.
2. FSLIC: This sign represents the Federal Savings and Loan Insurance Corporation, which is operated by the Federal Home Bank Board. The FSLIC insures accounts at federal savings and loan associations, federal savings banks, and state-chartered savings and loan associations that apply for insurance with the FSLIC and are accepted.
3. NCUA: This sign represents the National Credit Union Association, an agency of the federal government that insures accounts at federal credit unions and state-chartered credit unions that apply and qualify for NCUA insurance.

Figure 6–1. Maximum deposit insurance coverage for your savings

For a Family of Two

Individual Accounts	HUSBAND	Individual	$100,000
	WIFE	Individual	$100,000
Joint Tenancy Accounts	HUSBAND & WIFE	Joint	$100,000
Testamentary Revocable Trust Accounts	HUSBAND	Trustee	WIFE — $100,000
	WIFE	Trustee	HUSBAND — $100,000

Husband as Trustee for Wife
Wife as Trustee for Husband   **Total $500,000**

For a Family of Three

Individual Accounts	HUSBAND	Individual	$100,000
	WIFE	Individual	$100,000
	CHILD	Individual	$100,000
Joint Tenancy Accounts	HUSBAND & WIFE	Joint	$100,000
	HUSBAND & CHILD	Joint	$100,000
	WIFE & CHILD	Joint	$100,000
Testamentary Revocable Trust Accounts (for Spouse-Child-Grandchild)	HUSBAND	Trustee	WIFE — $100,000
	HUSBAND	Trustee	CHILD — $100,000
	WIFE	Trustee	HUSBAND — $100,000
	WIFE	Trustee	CHILD — $100,000

Total $1,000,000

For a Family of Four

Individual Accounts	HUSBAND	Individual	$100,000
	WIFE	Individual	$100,000
	CHILD #1	Individual	$100,000
	CHILD #2	Individual	$100,000
Joint Tenancy Accounts	HUSBAND & WIFE	Joint	$100,000
	HUSBAND & CHILD #1	Joint	$100,000
	WIFE & CHILD #2	Joint	$100,000
	CHILD #1 & #2	Joint	$100,000
Testamentary Revocable Trust Accounts (for Spouse-Child-Grandchild)	HUSBAND	Trustee	WIFE — $100,000
	WIFE	Trustee	HUSBAND — $100,000
	HUSBAND	Trustee	CHILD #1 — $100,000
	WIFE	Trustee	CHILD #1 — $100,000
	HUSBAND	Trustee	CHILD #2 — $100,000
	WIFE	Trustee	CHILD #2 — $100,000

Total $1,400,000

A resolution by the U.S. Congress, "reaffirms that deposits, up to the statutorily prescribed amount, in federally insured depository institutions are backed by the full faith and credit of the United States."

INSURED INDIVIDUAL ACCOUNTS

Individuals have available to them four categories of accounts that are separately insured. As long as the funds on deposit qualify for coverage under separate ownership categories, depositors can have insured accounts in each of the four categories in the same savings institution. The insurance limit is applied to the combined total amount the owner holds in all accounts within each category at the institution, regardless of the number or type (e.g. NOW, CD, passbook, etc.) of accounts.

Individual Accounts

Individual accounts are insured up to $100,000 in the aggregate. For example, if a depositor has both a NOW account and a Certificate of Deposit in one name alone, the funds in these accounts would be added together and insured for a total of $100,000.

Joint Accounts

To obtain separate insurance in the joint account category all co-owners should sign the signature card and possess equal withdrawal rights. Insurance coverage is then determined by applying the following steps:

1. First, all joint accounts that are identically owned (i.e. owned by the same combination of individuals) are added together and the combined total is insured to $100,000.
2. After step one has been completed, joint accounts involving different combinations of individuals are reviewed to determine the amount of each person's ownership interest in *all* joint accounts. Each owner's attributable interest in all joint accounts is added together and insured to $100,000.

Both step one and step two are always applied so that no joint account (or multiple joint accounts with identical ownership) can be insured for over $100,000, and no individual can be insured for over $100,000 in the joint account category.

Testamentary/Revocable Trust Accounts

A testamentary/revocable trust account is insured for each owner to $100,000 per beneficiary *only* if the beneficiary is the owner's *spouse, child, or grandchild.* The signature card or other trust documentation must evidence the owner's intention that upon death the funds belong to the beneficiary.

EARNINGS ON SAVING ACCOUNTS

Where can households earn reasonable amounts of interest and have access to money when it is needed? There are a variety of accounts that provide different levels of interest earnings and different rules on the availability of the funds to the saver. Households should have accounts that best suit their needs, distributing their funds among these accounts to meet particular savings objectives. Four of the most common types of accounts are negotiable order of withdrawal accounts, passbook and statement savings accounts, money market deposit accounts, and certificate of deposit accounts.

Negotiable Order of Withdrawal (NOW) Accounts

NOW accounts allow depositors to earn interest on and draw checks against the funds in the accounts. They are offered by many banks and savings and loan associations (S&Ls). Similar accounts, offered by some credit unions, are referred to as share draft accounts. Some depository institutions offer these same privileges in accounts called Automatic Transfer Service (ATS), where funds are automatically transferred from a regular savings account to a checking account as needed to cover checks written by the depositor. Businesses are not eligible to have NOW accounts.

Also available are Telephone Transfer Service accounts (TTS), in which the depository institution makes specific payments from savings as ordered by depositors over the phone.

None of these accounts has a minimum balance required by regulation. Many institutions, however, have their own minimum balance requirements, and deposits in accounts with higher minimum balances usually earn higher rates of interest.

On NOW and similar types of accounts, there are no legal restrictions on withdrawals made in person or by mail, messenger, or automated teller machine.

Passbook Savings Account

One of the most practical ways of monitoring your savings plan is to secure a passbook savings account that provides you with an itemized list of deposits and withdrawals and interest earnings, and a periodic balance of the account. This allows you to easily keep track of the progress of your original plan. There is nothing sacred about saving a specific amount during a specific period. It is advisable, however, that you save regularly. For example, if your account shows a savings deposit during ten of your last twelve pay periods, this suffices for "saving regularly," even if the amounts of the deposits vary significantly. On the other hand, if the most recent deposit was made three or four months ago, you should recognize that you are falling behind in your plan and reinstitute your program.

Of all the financial arrangements that give you an up-to-date record of your savings transactions while achieving the objectives of safety and modest interest earnings, the passbook savings account is the most appropriate. Money placed in this type of account is immediately available for meeting unexpected expenses and emergencies, and the funds are free from any withdrawal penalty and any risk of loss resulting from conditions in the financial markets. You can secure a passbook savings account from commercial banks, credit unions, savings and loans, and mutual savings banks. These four institutions are often referred to as "thrifts." Although most banks and thrifts are flexible on most terms of the passbook account, they are empowered to stipulate a minimum opening balance and require notice before a withdrawal. As a matter of practice, thrifts permit savers to open an account with $50 or less, and they rarely require that you give notice to withdraw your money.

Before selecting an institution for your passbook account, you should consider at least three factors. The first is convenience. If you have to travel a considerable distance or leave your job during working hours, you may justify postponing a deposit. This could lead to spending the money for something else, thus interrupting your plan to save on a regular basis. With this in mind you may want to select an institution close to your job, so you can make deposits during your lunch hour; or you may want to select an institution very close to your home, thus allowing a nonworking member of the household to make deposits without traveling a great distance.

A second important factor in selecting an institution for your passbook savings account is the likelihood that you may want to apply for a home mortgage or some other type of loan in the future. When funds for mortgages and other consumer loans become scarce, lending officers at most **depository institutions** often favor people who have an account with them.

A third factor to consider is the **interest rate** offered by the institution you're considering. Naturally, you want to make as much money as possible on your savings. However, you should weigh very carefully the difference in interest rates against the convenience factor and the likelihood of your obtaining a loan at some future time.

Although the thrift and banking industries in general have a very good record for safety of deposits, you are still well advised to keep your savings in an institution in which the maximum safety is guaranteed. This, of course, means keeping your funds in an institution in which the deposits are insured by an agency of the Federal government. Before you deposit your savings with an institution, make sure that you see on the premises a prominently displayed sign or logo that includes the letters FDIC or FSLIC.

- **depository institutions:** commercial banks, savings and loan associations, mutual savings banks, savings banks, and credit unions.
- **interest rate:** the price in percentage form paid for credit or the privilege of borrowing money.

Credit Union Deposits

As a financial instrument for a modest amount of savings, a deposit with a credit union is very similar to a passbook savings account with a bank or a savings and loan association. One major difference is that you must be eligible to join the credit union. A credit union is a nonprofit cooperative association of people with a "common bond." This so-called common bond can mean that the people are engaged in the same occupation, or organization, or even live "within a well-defined neighborhood." When you deposit your money in a credit union, you are actually buying shares, which are analogous to stocks in a profit-making corporation. Credit unions sell shares to their members and make loans to them. Because the earnings on a member's savings or shares are termed dividends, the return itself is referred to as a **dividend rate**, as compared to the term interest rate on a passbook savings account at a bank or S&L.

Nearly fifty-three million Americans belong to credit unions, which are nonprofit financial cooperatives owned and operated by members, most of whom share an occupational, religious or regional affiliation. The unions' nonprofit status and lower costs usually allow them to provide better terms on loans and savings than commercial institutions.

Although a credit union is referred to as a thrift, along with S&Ls and mutual savings banks, the rate of earnings on savings with a credit union is usually higher than that on passbook savings at these other two institutions. The dividend rate advertised by the credit union is not guaranteed, however, in most instances, the advertised dividend rate is the rate of return that a member receives.

If you can join a credit union, you might prefer this organization to a bank or an S&L as a place to deposit your savings for reasons other than a higher rate of return. One of these reasons, of course, might be convenience. Some credit unions maintain an office on the employer's premises. Some employers permit periodic deductions for credit union shares from employee member's pay-

---

• **dividend rate:** the annual rate of interest paid on passbook savings account.

checks. Another reason some savers might prefer to place their savings in a credit union is that many credit unions refund part of the interest paid by members on loans made during the year. The most common interest refund is 10 percent of the interest paid. A final reason some savers might prefer credit unions over banks and S&Ls is the feeling that such savings are used as loans to fellow workers, who may not qualify for loans from banks or other lending institutions.

Like passbook savings at banks and S&Ls, savings deposited with credit unions have maximum liquidity and maximum safety. You may withdraw funds from your share account at most credit unions at any time, without any loss of principal and without any penalty. Deposits in credit unions are federally insured up to $100,000 by the National Credit Union Administration.

Consumer-Type Certificate of Deposit

For the household with a modest amount of savings and no short-term expectations of needing such funds, the so-called consumer-type certificate of deposit (C-TC) may well be the best instrument for producing extra earnings from these savings. The C-TC formerly described **time deposits** with interest rate ceilings tied to the yield of Treasury securities and with maturities that ranged from one and a half to two and a half years. These provisions were ended on October 1, 1983 for all time deposits with a maturity of more than thirty-one days. Thus, a consumer-type certificate of deposit can be viewed as any time deposit with a maturity of more than thirty-one days.

While financial institutions can establish their own minimum deposits for the C-TC, anybody with at least $100 can get a C-TC in just about any place in the country. Most financial institutions are paying so-called **market rate** on these certificates of deposit; once you buy the certificate at a specific rate of interest, you will

---

- **time deposits:** funds that are deposited under agreement for a stipulated period of time.
- **market rate:** average rate of interest set by the major suppliers and users of credit.

receive that rate for the entire term of the certificate. You can withdraw your funds before the certificate matures, but you will incur an early withdrawal penalty of thirty days' interest earnings on certificate with maturities of one year or less, and three months' interest earnings on certificates with maturities of more than one year. Although this penalty is required by the federal government, it is deductible on your federal income tax. In addition to having the advantage of no federally required minimum deposit and no ceiling on interest rate earnings, the C-TC is insured by the FDIC for up to $100,000.

Another very important advantage of the consumer-type certificate of deposit over other saver's instruments, particularly U.S. savings bonds, is the flexibility in the payment of interest earnings. At most depository institutions, you can arrange to have your interest earnings paid on a monthly, quarterly, semiannual, or annual basis. If, for example, you are expecting an increase in your regular household expenses, you may want to receive your interest earnings monthly. On the other hand, if you are able to wait for an entire year before receiving your interest earnings, your rate of earnings will be even higher because the interest is compounded. Most depository institutions offer an **annual rate** and an **annual yield** on consumer-type certificate of deposits. The annual yield is always the higher of the two, but to receive the annual yield you must leave your interest earnings on deposit with the institution for the entire year.

Other Financial Instruments

In addition to the consumer-type certificate, commercial banks and thrift institutions are authorized to issue a financial instrument with no specified minimum or maximum denomination. But, if a bank or thrift institution issues an instrument with an unspecified denomination, it is also required to issue a $500 instrument. While this $500 instrument is not designed specifically for individuals or

---

- **annual rate:** the rate of interest to be paid over a full year.
- **annual yield:** the interest rate paid over a full year compounded.

households with modest savings, it is within the reach of many savers in these two groups who have previously held their money in passbook savings accounts.

Like the C-TC, the financial instrument with no minimum or maximum denomination is a certificate of deposit, but it has several characteristics that distinguish it from the C-TC. These characteristics are as follows:

1. no federally regulated interest rate ceiling;
2. a minimum maturity that gradually decreases to the maturity for all time or savings deposits, as of March 31, 1986;
3. additions to the certificate account permitted during the first year without extending its maturity, at the option of the depository institutions;
4. **optional negotiability**.

Although most of the financial instruments that small savers can afford are issued or sold by depository institutions, there are nondepository institutions that also issue such instruments, particularly those for which the outlay is no more than $1,000. Among these nondepository institutions are the investment companies that offer money market mutual funds (MMMFs). The initial investment for many MMMFs is $500. Another nondepository institution is the U.S. Treasury Department, which issues Treasury notes and Treasury bonds in minimum denominations of $1,000. Details on the instruments offered by these nondepository institutions are discussed in separate chapters. However, it is important to understand at this point that commercial banks, S&Ls, mutual savings banks, and credit unions are not the only places that small savers can turn to for investing their modest savings. Other institutions, such as brokerage houses and investment management firms, while having the image of catering only to big investors, are actually interested in accommodating small savers as well.

• **optional negotiability:** the choice of letting the owner of the certificate transfer it to another person through the proper endorsement.

Interest Rates and Early Withdrawal

Simple Interest and Compounding. The simple interest rate on deposits can be compounded. That is, interest can be earned on accumulated interest as well as on the amount initially deposited. Compounding can occur over different time periods, such as continuously, daily, monthly, quarterly, semiannually, and annually. The more frequent the compounding, the higher the effective yield or total earnings on the account.

Interest Rates and Annual Yields. When shopping for time deposits, households should compare the interest rates and effective annual yields stated by various institutions. However, negotiable orders of withdrawal (NOWs) and money market deposit accounts (MMDAs) have transaction fees that can offset effective yields to some extent. In the case of these money market accounts, interest rates can change on a daily, weekly, or monthly basis, with most rates changing weekly.

Variable Rates. If the depository institution pays a variable rate, this rate will usually be tied to an index that is beyond the institution's control, such as a Treasury security rate. The variable rate will float with fluctuations in the index.

Early Withdrawal Penalties on Time Deposits. If the depository institution agrees to redeem a time deposit (certificate of deposit) prior to maturity, Federal regulations specify a minimum penalty which must be imposed. The applicable penalty varies depending on when the account was opened as well as on the institution's own policy.

A depository institution is required to disclose the penalty it will impose for early withdrawal, which may be more severe than the minimum required penalty. Generally, the institution has the option of refusing to allow the early withdrawal altogether.

OWNERSHIP OF SAVINGS ACCOUNTS

The form of ownership of a savings instrument can be very important, particularly in terms of convenience to the household. There are three basic factors to consider when deciding the form of ownership of a savings instrument: the ownership of funds, the right to transact business, and the right to change provisions relating to the administration of the account. Important questions to pose about the administration of the account are as follows: (1) who may make withdrawals, (2) what form will the interest earnings take and how frequently will they be sent to the owner, and (3) where will the interest checks be sent if this is the form of payment desired. Answers to these questions would be different for the various ownership arrangements. The individual account, joint tenancy account, and the tenancy in common account are three different ownership arrangements.

Individual Account

In this arrangement, the passbook savings account or the C-TC is owned by one person. This person owns the funds, has the right to deposit, has the sole right to withdraw funds and receive interest earnings, and is the only one who can change account arrangements.

Joint Tenancy Account

This is an arrangement in which the account is owned by two or more persons. To emphasize one of its major characteristics, interested parties also refer to this type of ownership arrangement as a joint tenancy with right of survivorship account. Thus, if one joint tenant dies, the surviving tenants continue to have the same rights to the savings account as they had previously. The assets of the account do not become part of the deceased's estate.

In a joint tenancy account, the names of all the owners are listed in the passbook or on the savings certificate. Also, each of the owners must sign the signature card retained by the institution. To meet one possible objection by savers to the joint tenancy account, institutions typically offer two versions of the account, namely a one-signature or an all-signature account. The one-signature account authorizes any one of the joint owners to conduct transactions on his or her own signature. Under this version, for example, the check for interest earnings would list the payee as "Cecil Patterson or Vivian Patterson," thus enabling either spouse to cash the check. Under the all-signature version, the names of all owners would be listed as the payee, and all signatures would be required for such transactions as endorsement of checks and requests for withdrawal of funds. In all-signature accounts, if one of the parties dies the beneficiary of the deceased would be the succeeding signatory of the account.

Tenancy in Common Account

In this type of arrangement, two or more persons share in the ownership of the account in much the same fashion as they do in the joint tenancy account. The difference is that in the tenancy in common account, each person owns a separate interest. Thus, if there are two or more owners, each is assumed to own an equal share of the savings in the account. All owners must sign the institution's signature card, all must sign for withdrawal of funds from the account, and all must authorize changes in the account or termination of the account. If one owner dies, an equal share of the assets of the account becomes part of the deceased's estate.

U.S. SAVINGS BONDS

Buying U.S. savings bonds is one of the best ways of saving. This is why more people own bonds than any other security in America. These bonds are ideal for special occasions such as birthdays and graduation—the gift that keeps on growing! Savings bonds are issued and fully backed by the U.S. government, making them one of today's safest investments. There are no service charges when you purchase or redeem savings bonds, as there are with many other investments. If you sign up for the Payroll Savings Plan, you can save as little as a few dollars a week or up to $15,000 a year in any one name.

Where to Buy and Safety

Series EE savings bonds may be bought over-the-counter or by mail at banks, savings and loan associations, and other financial institutions qualified as issuing agents, or from Federal Reserve banks and branches, and the Bureau of Public Debt, Washington, D.C. 20226. These bonds may also be purchased on a regular basis through the Payroll Savings Plan offered by many employers or the Bond-A-Month Plan offered by many banks.

If bonds are lost, stolen, damaged or destroyed, you should

notify the Bureau of the Public Debt, 200 Third Street, Parkersburg, W.V. 26101. Where possible, you should include serial numbers, issue dates, name and addresses on Bonds, social security or employer identification numbers.

Price and Purchases

The price you pay for a savings bond is half the bond's face value. Savings bonds are available in eight denominations, from $50 to $10,000.

Denomination	Purchase Price (half face value)
$ 50	$ 25
75	37.50
100	50
200	100
500	250
1,000	500
5,000	2,500
10,000	5,000

The limitation on the purchase of EE savings bonds is $30,000 face amount ($15,000 issue price). This limit governs the amount of bonds which may be purchased in the name of any one person in any one calendar year. In computing the limit, bonds registered in co-ownership form may be applied to the holdings of either co-owner, or apportioned between them, up to a maximum of $60,000 face amount ($30,000 issue price). For purposes of the limit, bonds registered in beneficiary form are applied wholly to the owner's holdings. No limit applies to HH bonds received in exchange for E bonds/EE Bonds/savings notes, or through the authorized reinvestment of the redemption proceeds of matured Series H bonds.

Interest Earnings and Rates

The difference between the price paid for EE savings bonds and the redemption value is interest. Interest is collected at redemption. Currently, bonds are guaranteed for at least twelve years from issue date, at a guarantee of 6 percent. In other words, the owners of EE

Savings Bonds will double their money, at the current guaranteed minimum rate of 6 percent, if they hold the bonds for 12 years. If rates paid are higher than 6 percent, the maturity will remain the same and a Bond will be worth more than the face value at maturity.

Beginning with EE bonds issued November 1, 1986, the minimum rate for bonds held five years or longer is 6 percent. Older bonds will retain their previously-guaranteed minimums until the end of their original or extended maturity period in effect October 31, 1986. These bonds assume the minimum rate in effect for new issues when they enter their next extension period.

When held for at least five years, Series EE U.S. savings bonds earn market-based interest or a guaranteed minimum of 6 percent, whichever is higher. The market-based rate, announced each May 1 and November 1, is 85 percent of the market average on five-year Treasury securities. These bonds pay interest by increasing in value. Their value at their maturity will be at least the face amount and more if the market-based rate is higher than the guaranteed minimum. Bonds issued before November 1982 will accrue market-based interest beginning with the first interest date on or after November 1, 1987. Bonds more than 40 years old no longer earn interest and should be redeemed (see exhibit 6–2).

Redemption

At the owner's option, Series EE savings bonds may be redeemed six months from date of issue at most banks and other financial institutions. If a bond is held for less than five years, an interest scale is applied, approximately as follows:

after one year 4.3%
after two years 4.6%
after three years 5.0%
after four years 5.5%
after five years 6.0%

Series HH bonds may be redeemed at any Federal Reserve bank or branch, or at the Bureau of the Public Debt, six months from date of issue.

Exhibit 6–2.   Guaranteed Minimum Rates for Series EE and E Savings Bonds and U.S. Savings Notes (As of December 31, 1986)

Issue Date	Original Maturity Period	Guaranteed Minimum Through Current Maturity Period	Next Extension Begins*	Current Life of Bond
Series EE				
Nov. 1986–	12 years	6.0	**	12 years
Nov. 1982–Oct. 1986	10 years	7.5	**	10 years
May 1981–Oct. 1982	8 years	9.0	**	8 years
Nov. 1980–Apr. 1981	9 years	8.94	**	9 years
May thru Oct. 1980	11 years	8.86	**	11 years
Jan. thur Apr. 1980	11 years	8.77	**	11 years
Series E				
Nov. 1977–June 1980	5 years	7.5	Nov. 1992–June 1995	25 years
Dec. 1973–Oct. 1977	5 years	8.5	Dec. 1988–Oct. 1992	25 years
Mar. 1971–Nov. 1973	5 years, 10 mos.	8.5	Jan. 1987–Sep. 1989	25 years, 10 mos.
Jan. 1971–Feb. 1971	5 years, 10 mos.	6.0	Nov. 1996–Dec. 1996†	25 years, 10 mos.
June 1969–Dec. 1970	5 years, 10 mos.	7.5	Apr. 1995–Oct. 1996†	25 years, 10 mos.
Dec. 1965–May 1969	7 years	7.5	Dec. 1992–May 1996†	27 years
Feb. 1965–Nov. 1965	7 years, 9 mos.	7.5	Nov. 1992–Aug. 1993	37 years, 9 mos.
June 1959–Jan. 1965	7 years, 9 mos.	8.5	Mar. 1987–Oct. 1992	37 years, 9 mos.
Feb. 1958–May 1959	8 years, 11 mos.	8.5	Jan. 1987–Apr. 1988	38 years, 11 mos.
Dec. 1957–Jan. 1958	8 years, 11 mos.	6.0	***	38 years, 11 mos.
Feb. 1957–Nov. 1957	8 years, 11 mos.	7.5	***	38 years, 11 mos.
Mar. 1953–Jan. 1957	9 years, 8 mos.	7.5	***	39 years, 8 mos.
May 1952–Feb. 1953	9 years, 8 mos.	8.5	***	39 years, 8 mos.
Nov. 1947–Apr. 1952	10 years	8.5	***	40 years
Jan. 1947–Oct. 1947	10 years ††	8.5	***	40 years
May 1941–Dec. 1946	10 years	†††		40 years
Savings Notes				
May 1968–Oct. 1970	4 years, 6 mos.	7.5	***	24 years, 6 mos.
May 1967–Apr. 1968	4 years, 6 mos.	8.5	***	24 years, 6 mos.

   * All bonds will earn 6.0% as a minimum when they enter their next extended-maturity periods.

  ** The Treasury will decide on extensions for Series EE bonds later in this decade as these bonds approach the end of their original maturity periods.

 *** Bonds and notes issued during this period already are in their last extended-maturity periods.

   † Extended-maturity periods would begin on these dates if extended earning is authorized by the Treasury.

  †† Bonds issued during this period will cease earning interest before November, 1987, and are not eligible for market-based interest.

 ††† Bonds issued during this period have reached final maturity and are no longer earning interest.

Exchange For Series HH Bonds

Series HH bonds may be purchased in exchange for outstanding Series EE and E bonds and savings notes (Freedom Shares). EE bonds are eligible for exchange six months after issue; E bonds remain eligible for exchange for one year after final maturity. Bonds/notes submitted in exchange must have a combined current redemption value of $500 or more. Owners who have deferred reporting, for federal tax purposes, the interest as it accrued on the securities exchanged may continue to defer such reporting to the taxable year in which the HH bonds received in exchange are redeemed, disposed of, or reach final maturity, whichever comes first. (See Department of Treasury Circular, Public Debt Series No. 2–80, for rules governing this exchange offering.)

Series H bonds cannot be exchanged for Series HH bonds, and should be redeemed as they reach final maturity. At the owner's request, the Treasury will reinvest the proceeds of the sale of matured H bonds in Series HH bonds. Reinvestment does not provide for the continuation of any tax deferral, nor is it subject to an annual limit.

Series HH bonds are issued only at Federal Reserve banks and branches and the Bureau of the Public Debt. Banks and other financial institutions will accept and forward exchange applications, and the bonds being exchanged, to the nearest Federal Reserve bank or branch. Delivery of bonds will be made by mail in accordance with the purchaser's instructions. Series HH denominations at face amount are: $500, $1,000, $5,000 and $10,000.

Registration

Series EE and HH bonds may be registered in names of individuals—whether adults or minors—in single ownership, co-ownership, or beneficiary forms; but only in single ownership form if in the names of fiduciaries and private and public organizations.

Bonds cannot be transferred, sold, or used as collateral. *Note*: If bonds are registered in co-ownership form, either co-owner may cash the bonds. For authorized reissue of a co-ownership bond, both must join in the request. If bonds are registered in beneficiary form, during owner's lifetime, only the owner may cash the bond. For authorized reissue of the beneficiary bond, only the owner may sign the request.

Tax Status

The difference between the price paid for EE bonds and the redemption value is interest. It is subject to federal income tax—but not to state or local income taxes. Interest is reportable as it accrues for federal income tax purposes, but such reporting may be deferred until the bonds are cashed, disposed of, or reach maturity, whichever comes first.

Interest on Series HH bonds is subject to federal income tax, but not to state or local income taxes. Such interest must be reported for federal income tax purposes for the year in which interest is paid.

Both types of bonds are subject to other taxes, such as estate, inheritance, and gift taxes—whether federal or state—but they are exempt from all other taxation imposed on principal or interest by any state, U.S. possession, or local taxing authority. Complete information regarding the tax status of Series EE and HH bonds is found in Department of the Treasury Circulars, Public Debt Series No. 1–80 (Series EE) and No. 2–80 (Series HH), latest revisions.

INCREASED BASE FOR EXTRA EARNINGS

Producing extra earnings from savings can be the most crucial aspect of a money management program for a household with very limited income and resources. After all, extra earnings mean that the household has additional income at its disposal, and in the long run this translates into a higher standard of living. No doubt some of this increased income will and should be spent on goods and services that can bring additional comfort and satisfaction to members of the household. However, a portion should be used to increase the base for producing extra earnings. If the household's rate of savings from wages or salaries continues at the same pace, the extra earnings should enable the household not only to buy financial instruments with higher minimum denominations, but also to advance more rapidly to the stage in which the household can consider more substantial investments with higher potential yields.

If extra earnings from savings are produced in a manner

suggested in this chapter, another important gain accrues to the household's program in money management—namely, confidence in the program. The extra earnings constitute visible evidence that a serious money management program can succeed in a household with limited income and resources. In addition, the strategy for producing these extra earnings, as offered in this chapter, demonstrates that this success can be achieved with minimum effort and virtually no risk.

7·

Fundamentals Of Investment

For many people, the months of August and September of 1981 produced the biggest paydays of their lives. During this two-month period, newly issued thirteen-week and twenty-six-week Treasury bills reached investment rates of 16.73 percent and 17.47 percent, respectively; money market mutual funds quoted yields between 17 and 18 percent; and money market CDs issued by S&Ls reached a record high of 16.09 percent. With interest rates expected to peak shortly thereafter, people who opted for longer-term securities did even better. Some corporate bonds offered an 18 percent return for thirty years; auctions of newly issued two, four, five, and nine-and-a-half-year Treasury notes brought record yields of 16 percent plus; and the thirty-month small savers CDs issued by S&Ls hit a record interest rate of 16.55 percent. Even stockholders shared in the prosperity during this two-month period. The stock market itself fluctuated, but holders of selected stocks reaped tremendous gains from the premium prices offered by giant corporations in their efforts to take over other giant corporations. After this burst of record-setting yields on financial instruments, it was no surprise that more and more people began to ask, "When should I start thinking about making a few investments?"

The precise point at which you and your household should start to think about investing is a topic that was partly addressed in the previous chapter. In essence, there are three stages for the deployment of savings, with the last stage leading into the world of investments. The stages may be summarized as follows:

Stage 1: Money should be put, and kept, in a passbook savings account for emergencies and certain designated future expenditures.

Stage 2: After the first stage is satisfied, additional savings should be placed in financial instruments that carry maximum safety, but yield a higher rate of earnings than the passbook account. It is assumed that earnings from these instruments will have an impact on what the household will or will not spend from its total income.

Stage 3: When the earnings from savings reach the point where any further earnings will not affect the household's budget, additional savings may be placed in investments. In this context, investments are financial instruments that carry risk, are not easily converted into cash, and have potential yields that are unlimited.

READINESS FOR INVESTMENT

Before you actually invest anything, you should have a readiness to invest. This does not simply mean having a desire to invest. Overall readiness includes an appreciation for—and a thorough understanding of—personal money management; a firmly secured financial base for the family; and certain intangibles, such as the investor's own mental attitude and his or her motive for wanting to invest.

It is essential to understand all aspects of personal money management before beginning to invest. Otherwise, you can't make the decisions required to amass enough funds to invest, or to know what to invest in. Personal money management techniques will give you a solid financial base so that investing will not be detrimental to your family's welfare. It is important to advance through stages one and two of a savings campaign before launching into investments. This sequence of savings assures that you and the members of your household can continue on a solid financial footing, even if an investment fails.

The investor's mental attitude, as a part of the readiness for investment, may be explained simply as the ability of the investor to accept bad news as well as good news. All investments carry some risk; some investments, such as stocks and bonds, involve considerable risk. So before you start investing, you should consider seriously whether you have the temperament needed to cope with a situation in which you might lose all the money you invest.

Although an individual's inner motive for investment is perhaps the most intangible of these readiness components, it is by no means the least important. When asked the reason for wanting to make certain investments, people are quick to cite such objectives as the desire for more immediate income or the need to put away something for the future. Fortunately, most people are sincere when giving these responses. There are cases, however, when the real motive of the investor is the mistaken notion that a person can "get rich quick" through investments. This attitude often brings disappointment to the investor and usually results in a financial loss by the members of the investor's family. Experience shows that there is no shortcut to wealth, and the investor who attempts to defy this experience merely proves that he or she is not ready to engage in investment beyond the point of having a passbook savings account or buying United States savings bonds.

WIDENED DOOR FOR INVESTORS

At one time, the "readiness-for-investment" concept also included needing a minimum amount of money to invest, and that amount was very high relative to what the average wage earner could hope to save within a reasonable period of time. Thus, until recently, only the well-to-do were able to consider more substantial investments, namely, those with potential yields that ranged from the market rate to rates regarded as extremely profitable. To be sure, there are still many investments for which the minimum outlay is five figures. However, there are an increasing number of investment opportunities in which you can start with as little as $100, and many such opportunities—the money market mutual funds, for example—can provide the investor with a market rate of return.

Another feature of most investments in past years was long payoff periods during which the investor would have to wait to receive any cash earnings from the investment—in some instances up to five years. In the past, too, many investments were marked by low liquidity. If an investor met with a serious emergency and needed all the funds that he or she could raise, it could take weeks, sometimes months, before certain investments could be converted into cash.

Today, if you buy $1,000-denomination Treasury notes or Treasury bonds, you can authorize a broker to sell the instrument and give you a check within minutes.

Closely related to problems of long payoffs and low liquidity was the lack of options among investment maturities. Years ago, the most prominent investments among financial instruments were stocks and bonds. Stocks have no maturities, and most bonds have maturities of ten, twenty, or thirty years. Today, an investor may select a CD with a maturity ranging from six months to five years, or a treasury security with a maturity ranging from a three-month Treasury bill to a thirty-year Treasury bond.

Another barrier to investments in the past was the lack of access to investments. Most of the firms offering investments were concentrated in the small downtown areas of certain cities. This situation has changed, partly because of the sheer increase in the number of firms offering investments and the development of multiple market areas. For the most part, however, this change in accessibility is due to the use of new marketing techniques by firms handling investments. These firms have not only brought invest-ment opportunities to the doorstep of potential investors by placing offices in hotels and motels, but have arranged for investments to be made by telephone, by mail, and soon by home computer.

KEY PRINCIPLES OF INVESTMENT

Though the doors have been widened for investors, in the sense that more people can become investors, such a development is meaning-less—and can in fact be harmful—if the new entrants do not have a reasonable understanding of the principles of investing. As in other activities, there are numerous principles and types of investments, and it is to the investor's advantage to understand and appreciate all of them. Two key principles are: first, decide what level of risk you are willing to subject yourself to, and second, analyze carefully the nature of the investment you're considering.

Risk

The possibility of incurring a loss from investing is commonly referred to as a risk. Investing involves risk because it is done with the expectation of reaping certain benefits in the future. Because the future itself is uncertain, the expected benefits may or may not materialize. It is quite rational for the investor to seek a high rate of return on an investment. In doing so, however, he or she should always be aware of one of the key principles of investment: the higher the potential rate of return on the investment, the greater the risk.

Risk in investment cannot be removed entirely, but investors can avoid some of the problems associated with risk. For example, after reading this book, investors should understand that risk varies widely among the different types of investments. They should also be able to recognize whether they are taking a very high and needless risk with a particular investment. Categories of risk and examples of investments that fall within these categories may be described as follows:

1. *Virtually no risk.* Treasury securities and CDs insured by federal agencies offered by banks, S&Ls, and credit unions.
2. *Minimal risk.* General obligation bonds of states and subdivisions.
3. *Low risk.* Money market mutual funds that invest in high quality money market instruments; corporate bonds secured by plant and equipment.
4. *Average risk.* Top rate revenue bonds issued by states and subdivisions; debentures issued by top rated corporations.
5. *High risk.* Low quality revenue bonds; debenture bonds issued by unknown corporations; stocks of small and new corporations, particularly new corporations in a declining industry or an industry in which the current firms are experiencing difficulties.

In the last three categories, the degree of risk can vary significantly within each group of securities, depending on the issuing organization. For example, corporate bonds secured by the plant and equipment of a firm that has sustained a series of financial losses may be very risky. You may receive your interest payments during the first few years, but if the losses continue, the firm is likely to go bankrupt, in which case you will not recoup any part of your investment. On the other hand, there are some revenue bonds that have a very low risk. Revenue bonds issued by states to build college dormitories, for example, have a very good reputation for meeting interest payments on time and returning the principal on schedule.

Nature of Investment

In addition to the risk factor, there are several other features that you should note when choosing a financial instrument for investment. One method of noting various features is to ask yourself such questions as: Do I want to become a part owner and reap the potential of unlimited earnings that go with ownership in a free enterprise economy? Would I prefer to be a creditor and thus have more assurance of receiving my earnings? Is now the time to make a long term investment? Do I want an investment that has growth possibilities or do I want maximum earnings immediately? The answers to these questions may not only guide you in the nature of your investments, but also confirm some of the goals and objectives set forth in your plans for personal money management.

Ownership.   Most investors like the idea of having corporate stock among their investments, thus becoming a stockholder. This is understandable because stocks have features that are sufficiently varied to accommodate many of the goals and objectives that the investor has in mind. As an investor, however, you should ask yourself whether you really want to assume the risk that accompanies ownership of a business, whether you are willing to search for all of the relevant information on a firm before assuming part of its ownership, whether you plan to exercise all of the rights of your ownership, and whether you are willing to monitor the value of your ownership. Many of the details on how an investor can carry out these responsibilities will be discussed in the chapter on stocks. It is important at this point, however, to distinguish an investment that represents ownership from other kinds of investments, particularly one that represents debt.

As an owner, you can expect your rewards to come in three basic forms: dividends, gains from selling your stock, and certain psychological benefits. Most beginning investors look for rewards in the first and third forms. Sophisticated investors look for their rewards in the first and second forms, but mostly in the second form.

Aside from utility company stocks and a very few others, income from dividends on most stocks does not provide a good return on investment. The income yield on most stocks is less than half the return that you can get from the ownership of Treasury securities, certain CDs from financial institutions, and top rated corporate bonds. Thus if the investor is looking for current income, ownership may not be the best form of investment.

Above all, you as an investor should avoid choosing the ownership form of investment for the pure sake of being able to say, "I own fifty shares of XYZ stock (well-known company)." Investment made for this purpose is a waste of money, and your remarks will most likely be taken as boasting, thus causing ill will instead of bringing prestige.

Creditor.   Whenever you invest in Treasury securities, CDs from depository institutions, corporate bonds, or municipal bonds, you are in fact a **creditor**. Being a creditor also carries risk, and, as in the case of stocks, credit instruments as investments carry various degrees of risk depending on the issuing organization. As a general proposition, however, having an investment as a creditor carries less risk than having an investment as an owner.

For the most part, an investment in a credit instrument does not require the kind of responsibility that an investment for ownership does. The exceptions might be an investment in the bonds of an unknown corporation or an investment in certain kinds of revenue bonds. When considering investing in these instruments, you should make a special effort to obtain all available information published by the rating service firms, such as Standard & Poor, Moody, and Dun and Bradstreet.

As a creditor, particularly as a bondholder of a corporation, you enjoy certain advantages over the owners or stockholders. A key advantage is that bondholders have a first claim on the corporation's income. In other words, interest payments are made to bondholders

---

 • **creditor:** one who lends money or permits another person to owe money to him or her.

before stockholders receive dividends. Another advantage occurs if the corporation is forced to liquidate. After the claims of such creditors as employees, supplies, and tax authorities are satisfied from the proceeds of liquidation, bondholders get their share of the remaining proceeds before any funds are distributed to stockholders.

Term. This element is the amount of time committed to an investment. Stocks do not require that your funds remain in the investment for a specific amount of time. All credit instruments, however, are investments for a specific period of time. While much of your consideration of the term of an investment should relate to your financial goals and objectives, your day-to-day decisions on this aspect of your investment should reflect your views on future economic and financial goals, and also your views on future economic and financial developments. For example, if you expect inflation and high interest rates to continue, you should favor short-term investments. If you expect prices to moderate or decline and interest rates to fall, then you should favor longer-term investments.

Many investors shy away from intermediate-term (two to five years) and long-term (six to thirty years) investments, with comments such as "That ties up my money too long." Avoiding intermediate or long-term investments could be a very wise decision. Then again, it could turn out to be a very poor one if interest rates begin to decline. There is no particular time period for interest rates to increase or decrease. You as an investor must regularly read the economic, financial, and political literature in search of clues on the direction that interest rates might take.

GUIDELINES FOR JUDGING INVESTMENTS

After you understand that investing entails some risk, that you as an investor can choose to be an owner or a creditor, and that the term of your invesment can be crucial to future earnings, you are ready to consider what you will require of an investment. In general, your investment requirements should fit in with your financial goals and objectives. However, to assure that all these factors are coordinated, you ought to recognize certain guidelines to be used in judging the merits of each investment and be prepared to compromise to achieve the **optimum value** from each investment. Experience indicates that the most useful guidelines for achieving optimum value are safety, liquidity, rate of return, capital gains, and tax liability.

Safety

As a guideline for judging the merits of an investment in a financial instrument, safety is related to risk. Risk is the potential for a loss, the possibility that the investor would not receive the return on the investment that he or she should expect under normal circumstances. Safety, of which there are different kinds, also refers to the potential for a loss, but goes much further by recognizing the different kinds of loss.

Safety of principal refers to the principal amount of the investment and addresses the possibility that the investor may not get back all of the original investment. If the investor is willing to hold an investment until it matures, then buying Treasury securities and CDs issued by insured depository institutions provides 100 percent safety of principal. However, no investment can assure 100 percent safety of principal if the investor is likely to cash in the investment before it matures. If a decision is made to sell a Treasury note or bond when interest rates are rising, then the investor is likely to get less for this note or bond than he or she paid for it originally. Also, if a decision is made to liquidate a consumer type CD before the thirty-month term expires, the early withdrawal penalty will result in lower proceeds for the investor than was invested in the CD originally.

Another kind of safety is associated with income earnings and logically refers to the possibility that the investor may or may not receive his or her interest earnings, and receive them on schedule. With most investments, the *safety of income earning* parallels the safety of principal. An exception may be certain revenue bonds that have

---

• **optimum value:** not the highest rate of return, but a respectable rate of return, in view of other desirable characteristics, such as safety, liquidity, and minimum tax liability.

not made interest payments on the dates shown in the bond agreement.

Even when a particular investment carries maximum safety of both principal and income, there is another kind of safety to be considered: *safety of value.* This refers to the degree to which the interest earnings and the principal will retain their respective purchasing power. To achieve a high degree of this kind of safety, the individual must have an investment in which the dollar amount of the principal and earnings has a reasonably good chance of fluctuating in the same direction as the general price level. With an investment in certain common stock, for example, this kind of safety is reasonably assured because the market price of the stock and the dividends will more than likely increase with inflation. An investment in a money market mutual fund would achieve part of the safety of value objective because the interest earning or dividends would fluctuate but the principal would not. On the other hand, many of the investments that would assure maximum safety of principal and interest earnings would not assure maximum safety of value. If, for example, you purchased a four-year, $1,000 Treasury note with a **coupon yield** of 13 percent, you would receive $130 in interest earnings each year and $1,000 after four years even if the rate of inflation was 20 percent in each of the four years. Thus not only would your interest earnings buy one fifth less in goods and services than you planned, but the $1,000 that would eventually be returned to you would buy considerably less than the $1,000 that you loaned the U.S. Treasury four years earlier.

Liquidity

In some respects, liquidity is closely related to safety as one of the guidelines for judging the merits of an investment. Liquidity refers to the degree that an investment can be converted into cash within a brief period of time without loss of principal. Most financial instruments have a reasonably high degree of liquidity, in that the

---

- **coupon yield:** the interest rate specified on the securities (notes or bonds). This is also referred to as the coupon rate.

investor can convert them into cash very readily. In the case of CDs issued by depository institutions, the degree of liquidity would never be 100 percent because the early withdrawal penalty would always result in a loss of principal. On the other hand, the liquidity of a CD is always considered high because the conversion into cash takes only seconds. Treasury securities are highly liquid because there is always a market for them. In most cases, however, the conversion to cash will take longer than a few minutes because it takes time for a broker or banker to find someone who will pay what the investor is willing to accept. Also, there is a certain amount of paperwork involved in processing the sale. With regard to the principal, the degree of liquidity could be increased or decreased, depending on whether the market price of the securities is higher or lower than the amount the investor paid.

It is advisable to have some portion of your funds in highly liquid investments. This would enable you to get cash immediately to meet serious emergencies for which your regular savings might be insufficient, or to take advantage of another promising investment opportunity that might arise at a moment's notice. With this in mind, you should make sure your investment **portfolio** contains a limited number of investments that may not produce the highest possible income earnings, but that can be converted into cash immediately, with ease, and with a minimal loss in principal.

Rate of Return

The desire to make money on money is the primary reason most individuals are interested in investments. One recent study on the motive for saving and investing indicated that the primary purpose is not to supplement current income, but rather to leave a "nest egg for the children." While this may be true, it does not diminish the saver's desire to get the highest return on his or her savings.

The rate of return is the relationship between the amount of earnings realized (interest or dividends) from an investment and the

---

• **portfolio:** the aggregate of investments held by an individual or organization.

principal or original amount of funds committed to the investment. Most rates of return are expressed and shown on an annual basis. This is true even when the maturity of the investment is one month, thirteen weeks, or some other period under one year. For some investments, the rate of return is stated explicitly, such as the 9 percent interest rate shown on a newly issued bond. In other cases, the investor may have to compute the rate of return on an investment. For example, someone may be offering to sell you a bond for $4,000 that has a principal of $5,000 and an interest rate of 6 percent printed on the bond certificate. In this instance, you would compute your potential rate of return on the bond by dividing the $300 in annual interest payments by your $4,000 investment. Your rate of return, therefore, would be 7.5 percent. The effective yield of 7.5 percent is higher than the stated rate of 6 percent because you would be earning interest as if you had paid $5,000 for the bond, rather than $4,000.

As an investor, you should always seek the *optimum* rate of return on your investment, and not necessarily the highest rate of return. To be sure, the concept of optimum rate of return includes the highest rate of return. But the idea is to earn the highest rate of return possible, given the level of safety desired and the priority placed on liquidity. As a rule the investments that promise the higher rates of return have less safety and less liquidity. These investments offer a premium that is intended to reflect the risk and degree of liquidity desired by most investors.

The rate of return also varies with the period of time for which the investment is made. Generally, but not always, higher rates of return are associated with longer periods of time committed to the investment. The element of time is actually tied to risk because the longer the investment is outstanding, the higher the possibility that something could affect the safety of the investment.

Capital Gains

A capital gain occurs when the investor sells a particular investment for more than he paid for it. Many investors regard capital gains as another form of income and a part of their total return from the investment. Thus, when these investors are structuring their investment portfolios, they consider financial instruments that are transferable or marketable, and try to purchase or invest those instruments that they feel have the best chance of increasing in value.

From the outset, it should be understood that no investor should purchase a financial instrument with a view toward making a capital gain unless that investor has the time and access to information that will allow him or her to monitor the day-to-day changes in its value. A few of the familiar financial instruments, such as the consumer-type CD, cannot be sold in the open market, and thus have no potential for capital gains. **Common stocks**, corporate bonds, municipal bonds, and Treasury securities, however, are transferable, and the market information on the changes in the prices of these securities is listed in most daily newspapers.

In addition to having access to market information on financial instruments, and the time to monitor the changes in their value as reflected by this information, you ought to have considerable experience in investing before you begin judging and making investments on the potential for capital gain. A capital gain can result from the purchase of an investment that is currently underpriced, such as stock, or it can result from circumstances that increase the value of the investment, such as the effect that steadily declining interest rates have on bonds. In either case, if you purchase the investment expecting a change in value, you should have the background, knowledge, and experience to make this type of judgment. For example, if the market price of "A" Company stock has remained virtually unchanged for a significant period of time, you may be justified in buying it as an underpriced stock if you know about some potential developments at "A" Company that other investors are not aware of. Accurately predicting those changes in interest rates that affect the value of bonds also requires knowledge of future developments.

Making investments with a view toward achieving capital gains is very risky, to say the least. Even if you meet all of the conditions mentioned above, it is still possible that the financial instrument could wind up losing value instead of gaining value. The ability to

• **common stocks:** securities representing an ownership interest in a corporation and carrying specified rights for the owner.

sustain a loss is part of your readiness to be an investor. However, you should always be aware of the factors that will enable you to minimize your chances for a loss.

Tax Liability

Although tax planning was discussed in detail in a previous chapter, it does not hurt to reemphasize that taxes should be placed alongside of safety, liquidity, rate of return, and capital gains as a consideration when you are making an investment. All investors are interested in increasing their earnings. However, they would prefer to increase these earnings with a minimal increase in tax liability. Previously, it was suggested that it may not always be in your best interest to seek the highest rate of return, because in doing so, you might be forced to sacrifice safety and liquidity. You may add to this the sacrifice of not minimizing your tax liability. Actually, you ought to consider the total tax liability—that is, federal, state, and local—on each investment in order to arrive at the highest rate of return.

Because of the frequent changes in the tax laws, it is very difficult to plan investments in which tax considerations will play a prominent role in the investment decision. For example, before the 1980 tax year, the Federal income tax law allowed a taxpayer to exclude up to $100 ($200 on a joint return) in dividends. For the 1981 tax year, the law was changed to allow a taxpayer to exclude up to $200 ($400 on a joint return) in dividends and interest. Starting with the 1982 tax year, the law went back to allowing only the exclusion of $100 ($200 on a joint return) in dividends and interest. Now, with the most recent tax legislation (the Tax Reform Act of 1986), the dividend exclusion is completely eliminated.

Many investors in the lower tax brackets do not feel that tax considerations are very important in their financial affairs, and many investors in the middle tax brackets ignore the potential impact of state income taxes on their financial affairs. Both groups should take a closer look at their tax liability, with a view toward determining the precise "dollars and cents" difference that would have resulted from another investment choice. Investment decisions should not be made solely for tax reasons, but before an investment decision is made, you ought to know how the decision is likely to affect your total tax liability.

INVESTMENT IN CORPORATE SECURITIES

When you consider buying corporate stocks and bonds, you should avoid decisions based on emotions, slogans, actions of friends, and your own ego, and give utmost priority to fulfilling your investment goals and objectives. Emotions and slogans do not produce immediate income, and actions of friends and your ego do not produce security in retirement. Immediate income and long-term security are two of the goals cherished by most investors, and if you are the typical investor, you should be reasonably sure that your purchases of any stocks and bonds are planned to fulfill one of these objectives.

Your investment goals and objectives may change as your family proceeds from one stage in its economic life cycle to another stage. Accordingly, you should purchase different stocks and bonds at different periods of your investment lifetime. For example, during the period when your children are at home or in college, your need for supplemental or immediate income is at its highest point. Your purchases of stock during this period should be concentrated among various utilities. Over an extended period of time, utility company stocks provide very little growth. However, utility stocks do provide a fairly good current yield in cash dividends, and they can usually provide very even growth in dividend payouts.

If you are keenly aware of your investment goals and objectives, there is nothing wrong with purchasing corporate securities. Many high-rate corporate bonds pay interest that is competitive with Treasury bonds, and therefore qualify as good fixed income investments. While the current yield of most stocks may not be competitive with the cash earnings provided by fixed income securities, there are times when individual companies generate very impressive levels of earnings. Their stockholders share this good fortune through increased dividends, stock splits, and market appreciation of the stocks. Unlike planning for the purchase of CDs from depository institutions or securities from the Federal government, planning for the purchase of corporate securities places a heavy responsibility on the individual to research the corporation, to monitor the movement in the price of its securities, and to know when to trade the securities. If you are ready to do all of this and do it thoroughly, then you are ready to consider the purchase of corporate stocks and bonds.

INVESTIGATE BEFORE YOU INVEST

Today, millions of citizens own corporate stocks, bonds, and other forms of securities or securities instruments. Many others invest in mutual funds as a way of increasing their wealth. Whatever the choice of investment, investigating before investing helps ensure that you have the proper information to use your funds wisely. The following are a number of rules that you should utilize in your investigation, and should generally observe in order to protect yourself as an investor.

1. Before buying . . . think!
2. Don't deal with strange securities firms. (Consult your broker, your banker, or another experienced person you know and trust.)
3. Beware of securities offered over the telephone by strangers.
4. Don't listen to high-pressure sales talk.
5. Beware of promises of spectacular profits.
6. Be sure you understand the risks of loss.
7. Don't buy on tips and rumors. Get all the facts!
8. Consult a person who understands all the written information if you do not.
9. Give at least as much consideration to buying securities as you would to buying other valuable property.
10. Don't speculate. Speculating may serve a useful market purpose, but only when carried out by those who understand and can manage the risk involved.
11. Beware of "confidence" schemes. If you're promised "quick profits," "a sure thing," "double your money," be skeptical and get in touch either with the closest field office of the SEC or with your State Securities Administrator, to help us track down crooked operators who deserve to be put out of the business.
12. Ask for information. Reputable securities salespeople will be happy to mail you a "prospectus" or "offering circular" on any

security that you're interested in. Ask for these documents and save the information.

13. Be prudent. Don't invest until your financial situation permits.

14. Follow your investments. After you've invested, keep on top of your investments. Read information sent to you by the company or companies in which you've invested. Look at statements from your broker. Overall, after buying . . . think!

The Investigator's Responsibility

In most instances, simply contemplating entrance into the world of investments means that you have already achieved considerable success in personal money management. It means that you have established a sound budgeting procedure, have provided your household with protection against emergencies, and have started to generate earnings from your savings. Continued success in personal money management as an investor will involve many more factors than you have faced up to now. Therefore, you should pay even more attention to such basic functions as planning, analyzing, and controlling your financial activities, in addition to carrying out the principles of investment.

In following through on one of your responsibilities in personal money management, namely, reviewing the financial literature, you will often read articles aimed at the investor. In some instances, these discussions will purport to inform you of the most recent developments in investments. In other instances, however, the discussions will amount to little more than an advertisement for a particular investment. This places the responsibility on you to separate hype from fact. You should always want to keep abreast of the investment world, but at the same time avoid enticements that claim to have already done the planning, analyzing, and controlling for you and your household.

INVESTMENT ESSENTIALS

Of all the activities involved in managing the household's financial affairs, none is more crucial to advancing the household beyond the mere subsistence level than investments. By the same token, no other activity can result in a quicker fall from above-subsistence level to subsistence level. For these two reasons, it is always advisable for decision-makers in the household to have certain essentials in mind when considering any action on investments. These essentials should include the following:

1. Never invest in anything that you do not understand.
2. Have some idea of how you will be able to sell or liquidate the investment before buying it.
3. As a short term objective, always strive to earn the market rate of return.
4. As a long term objective, try to sell your savings at a higher rate than you pay for the savings of others.

8 ·

Stocks And The Stock Market

Millions of citizens own stocks today because they know that in addition to receiving income on their investment, they own an asset whose value often keeps pace with the rate of inflation. When you buy stock, you are not only one of the owners of a corporation, but also an investor whose investment provides money for business growth, additional jobs, and an expanding economy.

To repeat an earlier word of caution, there is a difference between investment and other economic activities carried on by the household. For example, when you buy a car or a household appliance, you can examine the merchandise, compare prices of sellers, and have a fairly good idea of whether the seller is asking a reasonable price. When you buy a share of stock, however, you merely get a stock certificate. You obtain your certificate for a price that is difficult to compare with the price of certificates sold by other firms.

To be sure, there is a measure of protection for buyers of corporate securities. In terms of fraud, for example, the **Securities and Exchange Commission (SEC)**, a federal agency, has two basic responsibilities:

1. to see that firms that offer their securities for sale in "interstate

* **Securities and Exchange Commission (SEC):** the Federal agency charged with the responsibility of regulating the securities markets and all publicly held investment companies.

commerce" file with the commission and make available to investors complete and accurate information;

2. to protect investors against misrepresentation and fraud in the issuance and sale of securities.

Even with SEC protection, you are responsible, as a prospective investor, for seeking and analyzing all of the information readily available about the corporate securities you're considering. If this investigation is thorough, you will have given yourself some protection against being disappointed by a low return from your investment.

TYPES OF STOCKS

Corporations issue two basic types of stock to investors: **common stock** and **preferred stock**. Both represent ownership, although they differ in such matters as participation in corporate decisions, priority on income, and claim on the corporation's assets. They may differ in other ways, depending on the by-laws of the issuing corporation. In some instances, corporations issue preferred stock that may be converted into common stock at the stockholder's option. Both types of stock are often referred to as equities.

If you are not particularly interested in participating in decision-making at the corporation, and would like to avoid fluctuations in earnings from your stock, then you might favor preferred stock. Preferred stock carries a fixed rate of dividends that is expressed as a percentage of the **par value** of the stock. For example, if a share of preferred stock is issued at a par value of $100 and the stated rate is 18 percent, the stock is referred to as an "8 percent preferred." You

---

- **common stock:** securities representing an ownership interest in a corporation and carrying specified rights for the owner.
- **preferred stock:** corporate ownership that features a fixed dollar income. If the corporation has any earnings, this form of ownership has a claim on earnings and assets before the claim of common stock.
- **par value:** the face value printed on common and preferred stocks and bonds. As this is meaningless for common stock, most of this stock is issued as no-par stock of $1 par.

as the stockholder would be entitled to an annual dividend of $8 per share.

As an owner of preferred stock, you would also enjoy priority over common stockholders in receiving dividend payments and in claims on the firm's assets in case of liquidation. Preferred stockholders must receive their dividends before any dividends are paid to common stockholders. In addition, most preferred stock is cumulative, which means that if a corporation fails to pay the stipulated dividends to holders of this stock in any year, the dividends accumulate and the total must be paid before any dividends can be distributed to holders of common stock.

If you buy common stock, you can participate in corporate decision-making by voting on certain issues to be decided by the corporation. You are also betting that the company will enjoy rising profits and pay higher and higher dividends; that these increasing profits and dividends will eventually increase the market value of the stock, and thus allow you to reap a capital gain from selling the stock. This, in turn, would increase your assets and your personal net worth, which would mean greater collateral in case you want to borrow money. On the other hand, all of this may or may not materialize. There are many instances in which companies enjoy several profitable years but dividends remain the same. For example, a company may have a history of paying the same dividend whether the net profit for the quarter is $1 million or $10 million. There are also numerous instances in which the company enjoys many profitable periods, but the market price of the stock remains about the same.

Generally, common stock can be attractive as an investment if the composite return (dividends plus expected appreciation) promises to exceed the returns available on alternative investments, such as Treasury securities, municipal bonds, corporate bonds, certificates of deposit, and various money market instruments. As an investor, you should view the purchase of stocks in terms of your investment objectives, and then purchase stocks that fulfill these objectives. One common investment objective, for example, is to supplement the household's income. To accomplish this, try to buy the stock of companies with a history of paying relatively high dividends and paying such dividends on schedule. In this context, relatively high dividends refer to the dividend yield. The dividend yield can be computed by simply dividing the annual dividend by the market price of the stock. Utility company stocks usually have higher dividend yields than those of other stocks.

If and when you decide to buy stocks, you must be diligent in carrying out at least two responsibilities. Your first responsibility is to gather all of the relevant information on the company. Among other sources, this information may come from your broker or your friends and colleagues who own the stock you're considering purchasing. These and other sources, however, should be supplemented by your own research about the company and its stock. This research should include reading the daily newspapers, financial publications, previous annual reports from the company, and special briefings distributed by brokerage firms and **rating organizations**. Your second responsibility is to know when to trade or sell your stocks. Stocks purchased primarily to produce income may not always do so, and stocks purchased primarily to produce growth may not grow or appreciate in value. When you sense that such stocks are not fulfilling your objectives, trade them for stocks your research indicates can fulfill your objectives. Both the national and international economies can change very rapidly. What may have looked like a promising company two or three years ago may now look very different. The responsibility for knowing when to trade stock is a very heavy one. Mistakes can be very expensive, derail the achievement of your objectives, and lessen your confidence in investing.

STOCK QUOTATIONS, BUYING AND SELLING

After your research on a particular company convinces you that the purchase of the company's stock will further your investment objectives, you should seek information on the price of stock. The price, in turn, will help you to decide how much of the stock you should buy. Stocks available for sale are listed by the organized stock

---

• **rating organizations:** firms that operate investment advisory services. The firms evaluate the relative worth of particular securities.

exchanges in the financial section of many daily newspapers. Among the organized stock exchanges are the New York Stock Exchange (NYSE), American Stock Exchange (Amex), and sixteen **regional exchanges**. You may find the current price of a company's stock and other relevant information about the price in a typical listing by the organized exchange. A typical listing, along with instructions on how to read and interpret the listing, is shown in figure 8–1.

Figure 8–1.   Daily Stock Quotations in Major Newspapers

(1)	(2)	(3)	(4)	(5)	(6)	(7)	(8)	(9)	(10)	(11)
52 Week					*P/E*	*Sales*				*Net*
High	*Low*	*Stock*	*Div.*	*Yield*	*Ratio*	*100s*	*High*	*Low*	*Close*	*Chg.*
112 3/8	53 3/4	Ford M	4.00	4.2%	6	13524	95 7/8	93 7/8	95 3/4	+2

COLUMN	EXPLANATION
(1) & (2)	shows the highest and lowest price for which the stock has sold during the last 52 weeks.
(3) & (4)	carry the abbreviated name of the stock and the current annual dividend, if any, in dollars and cents.
(5)	provide the dividend yield based on regular cash and stock payouts (special or extra cash or stock dividends are not included in this yield), and the earnings yield based on the current price of the stock.
(6)	gives the price/earnings ratio of the stock based on 1986 earnings, and the current price.
(7)	shows the number of shares of this stock (in hundreds) traded that day.
(8) & (9)	show the highest and lowest price for which the stock sold during the day. These prices were 95.88 and 93.88 respectively.
(10)	shows the last price that the stock sold for on that particular day.
(11)	shows the difference between the closing price today and the closing price of the prior trading day. The stock increased two dollars per share from the day before.

Buying Stocks

For the most part, new stocks are issued to finance the initial operation of a company or to finance the continued and expanding

• **regional exchange:** any organized securities exchange located outside New York City.

operation of a company. In a few cases, the company may sell the stock directly to investors. In most instances, however, new stocks are sold through brokerage firms. No matter how you actually purchase the stock, you should request a **prospectus** from the company or brokerage house before buying. A prospectus is designed to provide information to help investors evaluate the merits of the new stock. The typical prospectus describes the firm, the securities to be issued, the firm's most recent operating statement and balance sheet, the regulatory bodies to which it is subject, the nature of its competition, and any current negotiations (labor unions or pending mergers).

You may purchase outstanding stocks from other investors or brokerage firms. If you buy directly from another investor, both parties should endorse the stock certificate and forward it to the firm acting as a **transfer agent**, with instructions to reissue a certificate in your name. When you buy stocks through a brokerage firm, the firm processes the transfer of ownership. Most investors—at least most new investors—pay cash for their stock and keep the stock certificates either at home or in a safe-deposit box. Investors who buy stock on the margin must leave the stock certificates with their broker. Most people who pay cash for stocks keep them at home. Theft is no problem, because the certificates are registered in the owner's name.

To buy the stock, you should simply authorize the broker to buy the number of shares you want at the best price available when the order is executed. Unless something unusual happened that day in the company whose stock you are buying, the "best obtainable price" the broker gets will vary little from the price listed in the stock exchange quotation. As an alternative, you can give the broker a maximum price that you will pay for the stock. This is called a

- **prospectus:** a document issued by a company and filed with the Securities and Exchange Commission to describe the securities to be offered for sale and under what conditions they will be offered, as well as the prospects for company performance.
- **transfer agent:** a firm, typically a bank, that is authorized by a corporation to administer and record the transfer of its stocks or bonds between investors.

"limit order," and you can tell the broker that the limit order remains in effect until cancelled. This authorizes the broker to buy the stock when the price falls to or below the maximum price that you have stipulated.

There is usually no minimum number of shares of stock that you must buy, but the paperwork in executing an order for 500 shares does not vary much, if at all, from that required to execute an order for 10 shares. Thus, brokers have minimum **commissions**, which means that it is disproportionately expensive to purchase a very small number of shares. A so-called round lot is 100 shares, and when you buy less than a round lot, you may pay a higher per share commission.

When you ask your broker about the prices of the stocks shown in figure 8–1, the prices at that moment may differ from those in the listing. The broker has access to the up-to-the-minute price or the market price of that stock. Let us assume that the price of a share of XYZ stock is $36.00 and the annual earnings rate is $3.60. This would give you a **P/E ratio** of ten. Stocks with a relatively high P/E ratio are supposed to have very good potential for **growth**.

Selling Stock

Knowing when and how to sell stock is just as important as knowing when and how to buy stock. Aside from the need for immediate cash, there could be a number of reasons for selling your stock. One reason might well be the stock's failure to fulfill the objective that you had in mind when you bought it. Another reason might center on an opportunity to buy other stocks that you feel have more potential for growth, immediate income, or some other objective that you consider when you purchase stocks. Suppose that immediate income is your primary investment objective, and that you are currently receiving a 7 percent yield in cash dividends from stocks that you purchased for $2,000—but the current market value

* **commission:** the broker's fee for handling a stock transaction.
* **P/E ratio:** price/earnings ratio; expressed as a multiple of the price of a share of stock to the company's earnings per share.
* **growth:** appreciation or increase in value.

of that stock is $4,000. Assuming that you know of other stocks or bonds that yield 7 percent, you could sell your stocks and use the $4,000 to buy some of the other stocks currently yielding 7 percent, thus earning $280 in supplemental income instead of $140. This is not to suggest that you should sell stocks simply because the market value has increased. In many cases, you may not know of a suitable investment to replace the appreciated stock. If the profit from selling the stock is relatively modest, and you decide to purchase more stock as an investment, the broker's commission could cancel out much of your profit.

Investors who become experienced in trading stocks, and who feel that they are very knowledgeable about current business and economic affairs, often attempt to reap a financial gain by **short-selling** stocks or making a short sale. In doing this, the investors essentially sell stock they do not own. They make such sales because they believe that the stock they sold short will decline in price. If the price does fall, they buy the stock at a lower price than they had sold it for, and deliver that stock against the short sale. In effect, the short-seller hopes to profit from a drop in the price of the stock.

To carry out a short sale, your broker has to be willing to lend you stocks that he or she is holding for other investors, and these stocks have to be ones that you think will decline in price. If all of these factors were operative, for example, you could sell ABC stock short, say, at $80 per share to Mr. Bull, who buys it because he expects the price to rise. Your broker would immediately deliver the shares of stock, borrowed from another customer's account, to Mr. Bull. You would then wait and hope that the price of ABC stock falls to, say, $70, so that you could buy the same stock at a cheaper price and replace the borrowed shares. You could cover yourself by buying at $70, and consequently make a $10 per share profit. If, however, the price were to rise to $85, then you would still have to

---

- **short-selling:** a technique in which an investor borrows stock from a broker in the hope of selling it on the market when the price of the stock is high, then buying it back when the price has dropped, and returning it to the broker after having made a profit.

buy the necessary amount of shares to replace the ones that you borrowed.

Needless to say, short-selling is pure speculation. You should attempt it only after you are very experienced in the stock market, have plenty of extra money, and have information that very few other people have. While purchasing stock for investment is also speculation, in the sense that you hope, but do not know, that the price will rise, such a purchase does not carry an obligation to sell the stock and thus risk a financial loss.

STOCK MARKET INDEXES

As indicated earlier, it is often difficult to measure the performance of an individual stock. It is logical to assume that if stock prices are falling in general, then a specific stock should also be expected to fall. The same logic should apply to a rising market. In an effort to try to track certain trends in stock values, several firms have established stock market indexes.

Among the most popular indexes are the Dow-Jones Industrial Index, Standard & Poor's 500, and the New York Stock Exchange Index. **The Dow Jones industrial average** (as the index is better known) consists of an average of the prices of thirty stocks on the New York Stock Exchange. These stocks are selected from those of large and well-established industrial firms. In contrast, the Standard & Poor's index uses 500 stocks, and the New York Stock Exchange (NYSE) includes all the listed common stocks on the NYSE—more than 1,200. Market analysts have varying opinions of the value of these three indexes, and each index has its critics.

The makeup of stock indexes varies over time. The New York Stock Exchange Index depends on what stocks are currently listed on the exchange. The Dow-Jones and Standard & Poor's indexes, though having fixed numbers of stocks, also change. Substitutions are made from time to time to better reflect the overall market. The

---

• **Dow-Jones industrial average:** number indicators of the movements of prices of certain groups of thirty stocks (utilities, industrials, transportation, and composite) on the New York Stock Exchange.

Dow-Jones index will be discussed in greater detail later in this chapter.

Most investors hear about the performance of certain indexes on radio and television each day, and probably think about how they can compare the performance of their stock with these indexes. Indeed, in some cases, a comparison is justified. However, before you make a decision to buy or sell based on such a comparison, you should make sure that your stock is very similar to the composition of stocks in that index. You should confirm your judgment by looking beyond the composite index and comparing your stock with that of companies in the same industry.

DOW-JONES INDUSTRIAL AVERAGE

Its True Meaning

Many of us hear a reference to the Dow-Jones industrial average several times a day. We hear it at the end of each news program on both the radio and television, and there are several references to it in the financial section of each daily newspaper. Depending on our work environment, we may hear statements on or inquiries about the Dow-Jones from our colleagues a few times or several times each day, and if we walk downtown where the financial institutions are located, we are likely to see one or more marquees showing the up-to-the-minute numbers on the Dow-Jones industrial average for that particular day.

For some people—many of whom are investors—all of these references to the Dow-Jones are either confusing or meaningless, or both. They are confusing to those people who do not know what the Dow-Jones industrial average is. They mean very little to investors who understand what the Dow-Jones industrial average is all about, but whose investments are not affected by this particular measurement of movement in the stock market.

Is It An Average?

As a starter, we should all understand that the Dow-Jones industrial average is really not an average in the true sense of the word. It is a figure computed by totaling the prices of the stocks of thirty companies and then dividing that total by an adjusted value.

The divisor is not the number of stocks (thirty) but a value that has been adjusted over the years so that the index is not affected by stock splits and stock dividends in excess of 10 percent. A stock split occurs when a company, feeling that the per-share price of its stock has risen too high for broad investor appeal, arbitrarily splits the high-priced shares into more numerous lower-priced shares. Say, for example, a stock is selling for $100 a share and the company splits it two-for-one. Other things being equal, the new price will be $50. Of course, each owner of the old stock must be given two shares of the new $50 stock so that the value of his or her holding will not be reduced. Over the years, each new stock split within the Dow-Jones industrial average decreases the divisor of the sum of the prices of the thirty industrial companies. Thus the Dow-Jones industrial average is not the dollar average of current market prices of the thirty selected companies. Rather, it is a market movement indicator, kept essentially undistorted by stock splits for nearly three-quarters of a century.

Origin of the Dow-Jones

The Dow-Jones industrial average, first computed on May 26, 1896, was based on twelve stocks. In 1916 the list was expanded to twenty and in 1928 to thirty. Over the years, a particular stock may for various reasons have become unrepresentative of a substantial sector of American industry. When this has happened, a substitution has been made and the divisor of the total of thirty prices has been adjusted, just as when a stock split occurs. On March 11, 1987, for example, Owen-Illinois Inc. and Inco Ltd. were dropped from the list of thirty stocks and replaced by Coca-Cola Co. and the Boeing Co. Inco had been a Dow Jones industrial stock since the list was expanded to thirty in 1928.

Is the Dow-Jones Useful?

The criticism is sometimes made that the Dow-Jones industrial average covers only thirty companies, and big ones at that, and so fails to reflect the movement of hundreds of other stock prices. But these aren't just thirty randomly-picked securities. The total market value of these thirty issues accounts for about one-fourth of the market value of all common stocks listed on the New York Stock Exchange. These thirty stocks are so widely held that they represent the personal interest in the market of a broad spectrum of the public. In adding Coca-Cola, for example, Dow-Jones noted that this particular company is not only the world's largest soft drink maker, but also a major factor in the entertainment industry through its Columbia Pictures unit and other television and motion picture interests.

If an investor is impressed by the movement of the Dow-Jones industrial average, he or she can invest in an equity mutual fund that invests in all thirty stocks. Many wage earners select these index funds as investments for their Individual Retirement Accounts (IRAs).

Other Dow-Jones Averages

Besides the thirty-stock industrial average, Dow-Jones publishes an average of twenty transportation common stocks (called the railroad average through December 31, 1969), one for fifteen utility common stocks, and a "composite" average of all sixty-five stocks. Also computed are six bond averages and one composed of yields on a group of bonds.

The function of all these averages is the same—to give a general rather than a precise idea of fluctuations in the securities markets and to reflect the historical continuity of security price movements.

STOCK PURCHASE PLANS

As discussed earlier in this chapter, stock is occasionally sold directly to investors, or more frequently sold through brokerage firms. In either case, you should always request a prospectus before purchasing stock. Fortunately, the Securities and Exchange Commission in a ruling in June 1987 decided that it has the authority to hold securities dealers responsible for the accuracy of information in a prospectus.

Sometimes you may be able to buy stock directly from the corporation. Many firms have stock purchase benefits that allow employees to buy the stock, often at a discount, through payroll deduction plans. In fact, some firms even match the employees' contribution toward the purchase of the firm's stock. The employee can often choose the amount of the payroll deduction made to buy the stock, and a brokerage fee is rarely charged.

Also, in some communities, public utilities have stock purchase plans for their customers. In Virginia, for example, one utility has periodically offered a plan in which its customers can buy the firm's stock with monthly payments over a twelve-month period. Interest accrues on the monthly payments, and the installment payments plus the accrued interest minus net expenses are used to purchase shares of the utility firm's stock. The installment payment for the customer has been as low as $10 per month.

While all of these special stock purchases plans appear to be very attractive, you as an employee or customer should still gather information on the firm and the stock before you participate in any plan. This holds true even when you are participating in an employee stock purchase plan in which the firm matches your contribution. In all instances, you should examine the firm's profitability record, the dividend history of the stock, and your ability to afford the amount taken out of your check to buy the stock. If a firm has a favorable record of profits and will match your contribution, then you might consider this an offer that you "can't refuse." On the other hand, if you are required to pay the full contribution, then you should examine several factors, including alternative investments that require the same level of investment. Remember, if interest rates are declining, the price of stocks begin to rise, and you should be wary of buying stock in a rising market. Most plans purchase the stock during a specified period, say, twelve months. This means that the stock is purchased at different prices. If the stock market is in an upward trend, the price will rise from month to month under the plan.

BORROWING TO BUY STOCK

Generally, there are two ways to finance the purchase of stock. One way is to pay the entire purchase price in cash. The other way is to buy on margin. When paying cash, you must pay the purchase price in cash no later than the settlement date (usually within five business days of the trade). When buying on margin, you open a margin account with the broker and pay part of the price of the stock. The broker lends you the remaining amount.

If you plan to borrow funds from a lending institution to buy stock, you should be well informed about the federal law passed by Congress, effective November 1, 1971. This law now requires the borrower, as well as the lender, to comply with the Government's rules relating to the use of credit in purchasing securities, even when the borrower obtains the credit outside the United States.

Before that date, the responsibility for complying with these rules was generally on the lender—a bank, broker/dealer, or some other type of lending institution. Now the responsibility for compliance is shared by the lender and the borrower. Borrowers who willfully obtain credit on securities illegally are subject to severe penalties. The maximum penalty upon conviction is a $10,000 fine and five years in jail.

The Federal Reserve Board, therefore, sets rules specifying the minimum percentage of the purchase price which you as a margin customer must pay in cash. Currently, the requirement is for at least 50 percent of the current market value of the stock.

Regulation X

The rules that borrowers must follow are described in Regulation X, issued by the Board of Governors of the Federal Reserve system. This regulation is entitled "Rules Governing Borrowers Who Obtain Securities Credit," and free copies are available at Federal Reserve offices throughout the country and most U.S. embassies abroad. Banks, broker/dealers, and many other lenders also have copies of the Regulation or are familiar with its provisions. Ask your banker or broker about them.

Margin Regulations—What Are They?

Since the early 1930's, the Federal Reserve has been directed by law to restrain the excessive use of credit for the purpose of buying securities. This is done by setting a limit on the amount of funds that banks, broker/dealers and others may lend on stock and convertible bonds. The limit is always less than the market value of the securities that are pledged as collateral. The difference between the credit value and the market value is known as the customer's margin. Margin regulations apply to transactions in stock and in related instruments such as options, warrants, and bonds convertible to stock.

How Margin Works For You

When you open a margin account, you will sign a "margin agreement" similar to an agreement signed to obtain a bank loan. This document states the annual *rate of interest*, its method of computation, and specific conditions under which interest rates can be charged. Interest is usually computed daily on an annual percentage rate basis.

When the Federal Reserve sets a margin requirement it is, in effect, specifying the minimum down payment that must be made in a transaction. For example, if the margin requirement is 50 percent, an investor who wanted to buy $10,000 worth of stock would have to put up $5,000 in cash.* The margin requirements would then allow this investor to borrow no more than another $5,000 from the broker to finance the purchase. Similar margin requirements must be followed if the stocks are sold short—when the investor sells securities that he does not own, in hopes that the price will decline. In the case of options, the "writer"—that is, the original seller—is also subject to a margin that is based on the value of the underlying stocks if he does not already have an offsetting position in those stocks.

The Federal Reserve regulations establish margin requirements that apply only at the time a stock is bought or sold. Therefore, if stock is bought on margin and its price subsequently falls, the regulations do not require the investor to put up additional collateral

---

* If he does not have the cash, he could satisfy the margin requirements by depositing stock collateral with a sufficient loan value. For example, he could borrow $1,000 by depositing stock having a market value of $2,000 (50 percent of $2,000 equals $1,000).

or to pay off part of his loan in order to restore the original relationship between the loan and the now lower value of the underlying collateral. Similarly, any increase in the Federal Reserve's margin requirement applies only to future transactions, so that an investor does not have to post additional collateral or pay off loans associated with margin transactions made under the earlier, lower requirement. However, most broker/dealers have maintenance requirements, and may require additional collateral or cash at any time. For example, the New York Stock Exchange requires its members to issue a margin call—that is, to call for more money— whenever a customer's net equity falls below 25 percent of the market value of the stocks held in a margin account, and many individual brokerage firms use maintenance margins that are somewhat higher.

NEW RULING AFFECTING MANY INVESTORS

There is another precaution associated with buying on the margin. This involves an agreement with a broker to arbitrate all disputes. The dictionary defines arbitration as "the process by which the parties to a dispute submit their differences to the judgment of an impartial party appointed by mutual consent or statutory provision." Many brokers will not accept a margin account unless the investor/customer signs an agreement to arbitrate all future disputes.

Before signing an arbitration agreement with a broker, you should consider two factors. First, you should understand that at the present, the arbitration proceedings are conducted entirely by the securities industry itself. Thus, the arbitrators are peers of the brokerage firm with whom you are having the dispute. Second, in a decision in 1987, the Supreme Court said, in effect, that if you the investor/customer, sign an agreement to arbitrate all disputes with your broker, you are stuck with the arbitrator's decision, with no recourse to the courts.

Despite the aforementioned precautions, buying on margin is still somewhat of a bargain under the Tax Reform Act of 1986. Under this tax legislation, you can still deduct interest on investment debt up to a certain point. Buying stock on margin is definitely investment debt. On the other hand, if you borrow against securities already in your portfolio and use the money for consumer spending, the interest is not tax-deductible.

Many investors are affected by the law and Regulation X. More than thirty million Americans own stocks and bonds, and margin credit totaling several billions of dollars is outstanding at any given time.

SELECTING A BROKER

If you are interested in buying stocks, choosing a broker is one of your most important decisions. As in other matters of buying personal services, it is advisable to consult your local banker and friends who use brokers. Some brokers have an excellent record of advising customers on investments and playing a key role in helping customers achieve their objectives. Other brokers are known for "churning," that is, advising customers to buy and sell stock frequently for the sole purpose of earning increased commissions.

Brokers do not all provide the same services, they do not all charge the same rates for the same services, and they are not all equally capable and efficient in performing those services. With over 5,000 persons and firms registered with the Securities and Exchange Commission as "broker/dealers," you can and should shop and compare before opening an account. If you are dissatisfied with the range of services provided, the way they are performed, or the rates charged, you do have other choices. While investors are most aware of the large, national firms who advertise widely and who provide a wide range of services, there are many smaller firms that render all of the services most commonly used by individual investors.

One factor to consider in selecting a broker is the type of services that are required. An inexperienced investor may want a "full service" broker who will provide securities research services and recommend investments based on the investor's individual situation. The broker will take into consideration such factors as the amount of money to be invested, the type of investment (long or short), and the estimated risks and rewards. Full service brokers also provide custody service for their customers and generally offer these customers securities for which they (the brokers) are underwriters or **market-makers**.

DISCOUNT BROKERS

After gaining some experience in buying stocks through a regular broker, you ought to consider reducing your commission costs by using a "discount broker." These brokers generally confine themselves to the execution of orders at the investor's discretion, and charge substantially discounted commission rates. They usually do not perform any research or other services for their customers. Investors who know enough about the market to decide which investments are best for them may need a broker just to execute their transactions.

Many commercial banks are now entering the securities business by offering discount brokerage services to the public. Banks can offer discount brokerage relatively easily because they already possess many of the facilities and resources needed to perform this activity. Banks have computer and communications systems, branch networks, staffs of trained personnel, and depositors who are potential customers. Since discount brokerage can be built largely upon existing facilities, banks can use this product to lower unit costs for the entire range of retail products offered.

In offering discount brokerage services, banks enjoy several distinct advantages over competitors. Some of these advantages are operational because banks can obtain capital at lower cost and have easier access to technological and managerial resources. They can offer more conveniences through their ability to deliver brokerage services through networks of branches and to settle securities trades automatically through bank accounts. Banks have a further marketing advantage over other securities firms because of their reputation for being safe, sound, trustworthy, and conservative. They can use their marketing advantage to sell asset management accounts that are similar to those of full service brokers.

• **market-makers:** brokers who are willing to buy back a security from a customer at a certain price.

9 ·

Commercial
Bonds

Bonds are long-term debt securities that are issued by corporations and various levels of government. Bonds issued by governments will be discussed in the next chapter. In effect, a bond is simply a written promise by an issuer to pay interest on a debt and the principal. When the investor buys the bond, he or she becomes a creditor of the issuer. All bonds have three elements: the principal, the term, and the rate. All three of these elements appear on the bond certificate. The principal is the amount of money that the issuer is borrowing; this amount is also referred to as the face value or the par value. The term, or maturity of the bond, is the length of time for which the principal is borrowed. The rate is a percentage of the principal, and is the fixed interest that the issuer promises to pay you for the use of your money.

After a bond is issued originally, the rate of interest and the term remain constant. Although the issuer is obligated to return the principal to the holder of the bond at the end of the term, the price of the bond in the marketplace is likely to fluctuate, reflecting changes in the market rate of interest and changes in economic conditions. Generally, bonds are issued in $5,000 denominations, although some have face values of $1,000.

Interest is usually payable every six months throughout the term of the bond. Thus when an investor buys a bond with a principal of $5,000, a rate of 6 percent, and a term of twenty years—assuming the investor keeps the bond for the full twenty-year term—he or she will receive interest income of $300 ($150 at the end of each six-month period) each year for twenty years. At the end of twenty years, he or she will receive the $5,000 initially paid for the bond.

TYPES OF BONDS

The two most common categories of corporate bonds are classified by forms of ownership for the investor and by kinds of collateral the issuer uses to secure the loan. For the buyer or investor, bonds are issued in two forms of ownership, coupon or registered. Coupon bonds, or bearer bonds, are always owned by the person who holds the bonds, or the "bearer." These bonds can be transferred from one investor to another by simply handing them over, which is one reason coupon bonds are so marketable.

Coupon bonds are so named because there are negotiable slips attached to the bond certificates. Each coupon includes the interest payment amount and interest payment dates. When the interest payment date arrives, the owner presents the coupon to the issuer's paying agent (usually a bank) for payment. When the maturity date arrives, the owner presents the bond certificate itself to the issuer's paying agent for the collection of the principal. Buyers of coupon bonds must make sure their bonds are kept in a secure place (preferably a safe-deposit box at a bank), because whoever has possession of the bonds is the owner.

Many investors prefer registered bonds because the name of the owner is recorded on the issuer's books. When registered bonds are issued, the ownership or title to each bond can only be transferred by proper endorsement, with signature guarantees. Interest payments on registered bonds are mailed by the paying agent directly to the owner of record. The owner of a registered bond is better protected against physical loss than the owner of a coupon bond because the legal title to the bond is recorded with the issuer.

There are two types of bonds that are identified on the basis of the collateral pledged as security for the loan. One is a secured bond, because the issuer pledges a tangible asset to insure payment. When the collateral consists of real estate, the secured bond is often referred to as a mortgage bond. If the assets are securities of other firms, notes receivable, or accounts receivable, the secured bond is often referred to as a collateral trust bond. When the issuer pledges no collateral, the bond is called a debenture. For the most part, debentures are issued only by well-known firms, because the only backing for the loan is the company's good reputation.

In addition to all the aforementioned types of bonds, there are also "callable" bonds. Callable means that the issuing corporation can elect to buy back the bonds from holders—at the face amount—before the date of maturity. If you ever own callable bonds, and they are called, you should return the bonds promptly, because interest ceases to accrue on them after the date of the call.

"JUNK BONDS"

Another category of bond is commonly referred to as "junk bonds." These are low-grade, "high yield" bonds that are rated as speculative by the major rating agencies, and are therefore considered more risky than high or investment-grade bonds. Lately, these low-grade bonds have received a lot of public attention because of their use in corporate takeovers. The fact is, however, that most low-grade or junk bonds are not used for this purpose. Corporations that issue low-grade bonds are firms that, because of their lack of size, track record, and name recognition, used to borrow mostly via bank loans or privately placed bonds.

Low-grade bonds have been around for a long time. In fact, during the 1920s and 1930s, about 17 percent of domestic corporate bond offerings (that is, new issues) were low-grade. Furthermore, as the depression of the 1930s wore on, many bonds that were originally issued with a high-grade rating were downgraded to below-investment grade. These so-called fallen angels were bonds of companies that had fallen on hard times. By 1940, as a result of both these downgradings and the earlier heavy volume of new low-grade offerings, low-grade bonds made up more than 40 percent of all bonds outstanding.

Historically, default rates on low-grade bonds have been much higher than those on high-grade bonds, lending credibility to the speculative rating of low-grade bonds. A recent study finds that between 1970 and 1984, the average annual default rate for low-grade bonds was 2.1 percent, while the default rate for investment-grade debt was close to zero percent.

The default rate cited above does not deter all investors, particularly pension funds, insurance companies, bank trust departments, and mutual funds. Perhaps these investors are aware that default bonds do not become worthless, but retain, on average, about 40 percent of their face value.

Although individual investors have not been solicited heavily in the past as a market for junk bonds, some underwriters have begun to issue such bonds in denominations of $1,000 in an effort to attract individual investors. If such a development expands, each investor ought to review his or her own investment objectives and portfolio for guidance on whether to buy these bonds. As an investor who is thinking seriously about an investment in junk bonds, you should be prepared to conduct extensive research on the firm that is issuing the bonds. It goes without saying that you should be wary of a firm that is currently experiencing financial difficulties. However, you may find it worthwhile to look at a firm that experienced financial difficulties in the past, but has made a turnaround recently under new management. You may also want to consider buying into one of the junk bond funds, where you would have the advantage of a diversification of junk bonds. Diversification means that the risk is spread over a number of bond issues and that the investor is less likely to lose all of his or her investment if one of the bond issues goes into default.

An earlier chapter in this book attempted to explain all of the various ways of deciding upon investments. This discussion, combined with information on specific investment alternatives, should enable you to make appropriate decisions about junk bonds.

PRICES, QUOTATIONS, AND YIELDS

When bonds are first issued, they are usually quoted as a percentage of the principal or par value. To determine the dollar price of a bond, simply move the decimal place of the quoted price one place to the right. For example, a quoted price of 100 usually means a price of $1,000. A quoted price of 104½ is a price of $1,045. Bonds selling at the price of the principal or face value are quoted as 100 and referred to as selling at par. Bonds selling above par are referred to as selling at a premium, and bonds selling below par are said to be selling at a discount. If market interest rates rise, the price of a bond will fall, because any potential buyer of the bond will want a yield that is in line with market interest rates, as opposed to the lower interest rate currently stipulated on the bond. If these interest rates fall, the price of the bond will rise, because the seller of the bond will want a price that compensates for the higher yield that is given up when it is sold to someone else.

As an investor, your problem in buying bonds centers on the timing of the purchase. Ideally, it would be to your advantage to buy a series of bonds when the interest rate is at its highest level; that is, if you are interested only in current income. This is very difficult to do, however, because no one knows for sure when interest rates will peak. You may try buying bonds immediately after the series has peaked. Even with this strategy, however, it is possible that the interest rate for this series will start rising again some time later.

If you are interested in buying a previously issued bond, you should be concerned about the current yield or rate of return to you as an investor. In this sense, current yield is the interest paid on the bond as a percentage of the current market price, or the price that you must pay for the bond. For example, an 8 percent bond selling at 100 has a current yield of 8 percent ($80 interest income divided by $1,000). The same 8 percent bond selling at 90 has a current yield of 8.9 percent ($80 divided by the $900 current market price).

There are thousands of different corporate bonds already on the market, and new issues are placed on the market almost daily. If you are interested in investing in these bonds, you should first check the issuing company's credit rating to see whether you will feel comfortable about its ability to pay the interest each year and to return the principal when the bond matures. There are several independent rating services, including the well-known firms of Moody and Standard & Poor. Most experienced investors accept the ratings by these two firms as a good guide to safety. The highest rating is AAA, next is AA, next is A, and next is BBB. There are some ratings below BBB such as BCC; however, bonds with ratings below this level would be too risky for an inexperienced investor.

RATINGS

If you are very concerned about the safety of your investment in bonds, you should give priority to the credit rating of the issuing company, rather than the type of collateral pledged on the bond. Some investors are wary of buying debentures because there is no collateral for the loan. However, if a company has an AAA rating, its debenture bond is probably safer than a secured bond issued by a company with a BCC credit rating.

Another guide to safety when you consider buying corporate bonds is whether the bond agreement contains a provision for establishing a sinking fund. A provision for a sinking fund requires the issuing corporation to set aside an annual reserve of cash from its earnings to insure there is enough money to redeem or repay the principal of the bonds at maturity. In return for this added safety, you, the bondholder, must be willing to settle for a lower yield than you would get on a bond without a sinking fund.

You can buy corporate bonds through your banker or securities broker. Depending on the issuing corporation and your relationship with the bank or brokerage firm, the transaction fee may be $10 to $20 per $1,000 bond.

"GINNIE MAES"

In addition to bonds issued by commercial and industrial corporations, you may want to consider investing in another category of bonds commonly referred to as Ginnie Maes. Formally, Ginnie Maes are Government National Mortgage Association certificates. These certificates are issued by a federally-chartered corporation that buys Federal Housing Administration and Veterans Administration insured mortgages from private lenders, such as banks and savings and loan associations. If you buy a Ginnie Mae, you are buying into one of these pools of mortgages, and as in the ownership of any mortgage, the income to you consists of two parts: interest income that is taxable as ordinary income upon receipt, and return of principal that is low in the first few years and progressively larger as the mortgage matures.

Income payments from Ginnie Maes are sent monthly. These monthly checks, however, are not all the same size. That is because many home mortgages are prepaid ahead of schedule, and with every prepayment, you will get a particularly large check—reflecting your share of the prepaid mortgage principal. Your later checks will be smaller, because you now have less principal at work earning interest.

As a result of this continuous return of principal, the value of your Ginnie Mae unit decreases each month. In other words, each time you receive a check, you are receiving repayment of a part of your original investment. You then have the responsibility of reinvesting this amount as soon as possible if you want to maintain the level of your current portfolio. The payment statement that you get with the check tells you how much of the check is interest and how much is return of principal.

The interest income on Ginnie Maes is subject to federal, state, and local income taxes. Although these bonds have a generalized guarantee by the federal government, they are not obligations of the United States—as are United States Treasury bills, notes, and bonds.

In the final analysis, Ginnie Maes are a good investment. They usually yield a better rate than Treasury bonds, and they are packaged now so that people with modest savings can consider them for investment. The federal guarantee does not protect your investment against intermediate fluctuations in value. If market interest rates rise above what your Ginnie Mae units are paying, the sale of your units before maturity would give you a loss. In other words, in order to get both your principal and all interest income due on this investment, you must hold Ginnie Mae units to maturity.

If you want to buy a Ginnie Mae directly from the Government National Mortgage Association, the minimum investment is $25,000. If you have only a modest amount of savings to invest, however, you can contact a broker and buy a part of unit trusts with a minimum investment of $1,000. You need a broker who can tell you how fast the mortgages in your particular pool are being repaid, and explain to you the type of risk you take if there is a change in the life of the pool.

10·

Government
Securities

Just as you can invest in corporate America, you can also invest in
the government of America. In this case, we are not talking about
buying equity, but about buying debt in the form of securities
insured by the federal government, state governments, and local
governments. These securities are government obligations or IOUs,
and in many respects are similar to corporate bonds. Bonds are long-
term debt securities that are issued by corporations and by all levels
of government. There are also short-term securities—bills and
notes—issued only by the federal government.

In the jargon of the investment world, securities issued by various
levels of government are distinguished by names other than the
name of the type of government. For example, all securities issued
by the U.S. Treasury are referred to as "governments." Those
issued by specially authorized agencies of the federal government are
referred to as "agencies." Securities issued by state and local
governments and their agencies are called "municipals." Most
individuals are aware that securities issued by the U.S. Treasury are
direct obligations of the U.S. government, which means that the
interest payments and the repayment of the principal are backed by
the full taxing power of the U.S. government. While there are also
securities issued by specially authorized federal agencies, these are
not direct obligations of the U.S. government; however, the interest
payments and repayments of principal are guaranteed by the U.S.
government, because Congress has authorized these agencies to issue
debt instruments. State and local governments issue securities with
different types of backing, which will be discussed later in this
chapter.

For most investors, the primary attraction in investing in government securities is decreasing the amount of income taxes the investor must pay on the interest earnings. By tradition, a given level of government in the United States does not tax the income derived from a debt instrument issued by another level of government. Thus interest earned on bonds issued by state and local governments is exempt from federal income taxes, interest earned on securities issued by the federal government is exempt from state income taxes, and interest earned on bonds issued by local governments is exempt from state and federal income taxes.

U.S. TREASURY SECURITIES

Securities issued by the U.S. Treasury are backed by the full taxing power of the federal government, and are virtually risk free. There is absolutely no risk with regard to receiving your interest earnings and the return of your principal; but there is a risk in the purchasing power that your interest earnings and principal will have once you actually receive them. This risk is called safety of value (see chapter 7). For example, in a prolonged period of high inflation, you would receive your interest earnings and return of principal on schedule. However, you would find that you would be able to buy less with the interest earnings and principal than you could have during earlier periods.

Although the interest earnings from securities issued by the U.S. Treasury (hereafter referred to as Treasury securities) are exempt from state and local taxes, such earnings are generally subject to federal income tax. Federal income tax provisions change very frequently. To know exactly what your tax liability is on earnings from Treasury securities, you should consult the Internal Revenue code for the current tax year.

An added advantage of investing in Treasury securities is that you can sell such securities immediately in the case of an emergency, because there is always an active secondary market for Treasury securities. For a fee, your local banker or broker will assist you in finding a buyer.

All Treasury securities are sold initially at auction by Federal Reserve banks, their branches, and by the Bureau of Public Debt,

Treasury Department in Washington, D.C. If you buy the securities directly from a Federal Reserve bank (branch or Bureau of Public Debt), you do not pay a fee. You may also buy these securities through commercial banks and other financial institutions, but they usually charge a fee based on each transaction and the amount of securities purchased. One prominent brokerage house, for example, charges a flat $25 fee plus 25 cents per thousand. Thus the charge would be $27.50 for a $10,000 Treasury bill, the minimum denomination that you can buy.

There are three types of Treasury securities, namely bills, notes, and bonds, and all three are direct obligations of the United States government. When originally issued, they are sold through an auction process. They are commonly known as marketable securities, because after their original issue, they may be bought or sold in the secondary (commercial) market at prevailing prices through financial institutions, brokers, and dealers in investment securities. Marketable securities are not redeemable before maturity unless by the terms of their issue they contain a **call feature** and are thus subject to call.

The primary distinction between a bill, note, and bond is the length of time—or term—the security will be outstanding from the date of issue. Treasury bills are short-term obligations, issued with a term of one year or less. Treasury notes have a term of at least one year, but not more than ten years. The Treasury announces the issue date and the maturity date with each new issue of bill, note, and bond.

Another difference is that Treasury bills do not bear a stated interest rate, as do Treasury notes and bonds. Bills are sold at a discount from par. The owner does not receive interest payments during the life of the investment. The difference between the purchase price of the bill and the amount which the owner receives at maturity (par), or when the bill is sold prior to maturity, represents the interest on the bill. Treasury notes and bonds bear a

---

• **call feature:** the right of an issuer of bonds to retire the debt issue prior to maturity.

stated interest rate and the owner receives semiannual interest payments.

Treasury Bills

These are short term securities with maturities of thirteen, twenty-six, and fifty-two weeks. The thirteen and twenty-six-week maturities are sold on the Mondays of each week at Federal Reserve banks, and the fifty-two week maturities are sold periodically. You can purchase these securities in person, or by mail by completing a form called a tender. If a letter is submitted, it should be typed or printed carefully, and should include the following information:

1. the face amount of bills desired;
2. the maturity desired (thirteen, twenty-six, or fifty-two weeks);
3. the mailing address of the investor;
4. the date and the investor's name below his or her signature.

The $10,000 minimum denomination for a Treasury bill is beyond the reach of the average wage earner and the household of modest resources. However, you could form a pool of investors to buy the minimum denomination. In certain communities, investors with modest resources belong to an investment club. If you decide to try this arrangement, the club must designate one or perhaps two persons as the owner(s) of the Treasury bill, distribute the interest earnings, and—most important of all—arrange for the proper reporting of interest earnings for income taxes.

The shorter maturities and higher yields of these bills, particularly during periods of rapidly rising interest rates, combine to make them a very attractive investment. But frankly, an investment in Treasury bills is not worth all of the problems associated with a pool arrangement. Other financial instruments owned in a pool arrangement may provide you with many of the features of a Treasury bill, but fewer problems.

If you are determined to buy Treasury bills through a pool arrangement, or if you are able to invest at the level of $10,000, there are some things that you now know. For instance, Treasury bills do not bear a stated interest rate. Your earnings are calculated by taking the difference between the price you pay for the bills and the face value of the bills (if you were to hold them until maturity). This difference is the discount, and will be refunded to you immediately after the auction. For example, you would receive a check for $274.50 if the auction price of the bill turned out to be $9724.50 for a $10,000 bill. This $274.50 check would be a refund and not prepaid interest. Your actual interest income would come six months later on a twenty-six week bill, when the bill matures and the Treasury Department pays you the full face amount of $10,000.

The results of the auction of Treasury bills are usually reported in the daily newspapers on Tuesday, the day after the auction. Most newspapers will report the yield at least on a discount basis. For example, if you actually pay $9,250 as the auction price for a $10,000 Treasury bill, the newspaper will report the discount rate yield of 5.5 percent. Because you are investing only $9,250 for six months, the $274.50 interest that you will receive at maturity actually amounts to an annual investment yield of almost 6 percent. The investment yield enables you to compare your return on Treasury bills with your return on investments that are sold on a discount basis.

Treasury Notes and Bonds

Treasury notes and bonds have longer maturities than Treasury bills. Notes have a fixed maturity of more than one year and not more than ten years. Most notes and bonds are not redeemable before maturity. Periodically, however, bonds are issued with a call provision as a part of the agreement with the investor. This provision permits the Treasury Department to redeem the bond before maturity. A bond with a call provision carries a call date in addition to a maturity date, such as in the following example:

August 15, 1994–August 15, 2002

Although August 15, 2002 is the maturity date for this issue, the Treasury department reserves the right to redeem the bonds at face value plus accrued interest anytime between the two dates.

For you as a potential investor, the most important feature of Treasury notes and bonds is that (with the exception of notes with maturities of less than four years) the minimum denomination of these securities is $1,000. You may balk at the idea of tying up your money for five years or longer, but there are instances in which a fixed rate investment can work to your advantage. There are times when the yields on these longer-term maturities reach historic highs. For example, the U.S. Treasury states the best investment ever made in treasury securities was the 15.75 percent annual return on the thirty-year bonds issued in 1981.

BUYING TREASURY SECURITIES DIRECTLY FROM FEDERAL RESERVE BANKS

When buying Treasury securities directly from a Federal Reserve bank, you should submit a noncompetitive bid, leaving the competitive bids to be submitted by the large institutional investors. With a noncompetitive bid, you are not required to state the price or yield that you would accept. Instead, you simply agree to accept the average price or yield established in the auction. As a competitive bidder, you risk paying more than the noncompetitive price if the bid is accepted, or not being able to purchase securities if the bid does not fall within the range of accepted competitive bids. Therefore, you should submit a noncompetitive bid, which does not specify yield or price.

A forthcoming sale of Treasury notes and bonds is usually announced in most daily newspapers (see exhibit 10–1). When a sale is announced, you may subscribe for the securities in person at a Federal Reserve bank (or branch) or by mail, according to the time limits set by the offering. The deadline is usually 1:00 p.m. Eastern Standard Time. However, noncompetitive tenders will be accepted even if received after the deadline, provided they are postmarked no later than the day before the auction. If you decide to submit a subscription letter, the letter should contain the following information:

1. home address and zip code;
2. telephone number;
3. amount of securities desired;
4. whether bid is noncompetitive or competitive;
5. preference for the form in which securities are to be issued (if preference is registered form, name(s) for registration and social security number(s) must be furnished);
6. whether the purchaser plans to take delivery of the securities in person or have them mailed;

Exhibit 10–1. General Pattern of Treasury Note and Bond Financing by Month

The following is the current pattern of financing for marketable Treasury notes and bonds. The events are listed in the order in which they normally occur. Treasury borrowing requirements, financing policy decisions, and the timing of Congressional action on the debt limit could alter or delay the pattern. This outline is provided solely for reference and is not intended to convey information about any particular Treasury security offering. The Treasury Department issues a press release announcing each offering. Current information on specific upcoming Treasury auctions may be obtained from a Federal Reserve bank or branch, from the Bureau of the Public Debt, U.S. Department of the Treasury, or from the financial press.

January:	Issue 7-year note
	Announce 2-year note
	Auction 2-year note
	Announce 3-year and 10-year notes, and 30-year bond
	Issue 2-year note
February:	Auction 3-year note
	Auction 10-year note
	Auction 30-year bond
	Announce 2-year note
	Issue 3-year and 10-year notes, and 30-year bond
	Announce 5-year + 2-month note
	Auction 2-year note
	Auction 5-year + 2-month note
	Issue 2-year note
March:	Issue 5-year + 2-month note
	Announce 2-year, 4-year, and 7-year notes
	Auction 2-year note
	Auction 4-year note
	Auction 7-year note
	Issue 2-year and 4-year notes
April:	Issue 7-year note
	Announce 2-year note
	Auction 2-year note
	Announce 3-year and 10-year notes, and 30-year bond
	Issue 2-year note
May:	Auction 3-year note
	Auction 10-year note
	Auction 30-year bond
	Announce 2-year note
	Issue 3-year and 10-year notes, and 30-year bond
	Announce 5-year + 2-month note
	Auction 2-year note
	Auction 5-year + 2-month note
	Issue 2-year note

June: Issue 5-year + 2-month note
            Announce 2-year, 4-year, and 7-year notes
            Auction 2-year note
            Auction 4-year note
            Auction 7-year note
            Issue 2-year and 4-year notes

July: Issue 7-year note
            Announce 2-year note
            Auction 2-year note
            Announce 3-year and 10-year notes, and 30-year bond
            Issue 2-year note

August: Auction 3-year note
            Auction 10-year note
            Auction 30-year bond
            Announce 2-year note
            Issue 3-year and 10-year notes, and 30-year bond
            Announce 5-year + 2-month note
            Auction 2-year note
            Auction 5-year + 2-month note
            Issue 2-year note

September: Issue 5-year + 2-month note
            Announce 2-year, 4-year, and 7-year notes
            Auction 2-year note
            Auction 4-year note
            Auction 7-year note
            Issue 2-year and 4-year notes

October: Issue 7-year note
            Announce 2-year note
            Auction 2-year note
            Announce 3-year and 10-year notes, and 30-year bond
            Issue 2-year note

November: Auction 3-year note
            Auction 10-year note
            Auction 30-year bond
            Announce 2-year note
            Issue 3-year and 10-year notes, and 30-year bond
            Announce 5-year + 2-month note
            Auction 2-year note
            Auction 5-year + 2-month note
            Issue 2-year note

December: Issue 5-year + 2-month note
            Announce 2-year, 4-year, and 7-year notes
            Auction 2-year note
            Auction 4-year note
            Auction 7-year note
            Issue 2-year and 4-year notes

7. address(es) for delivery of the securities and interest checks;
8. purchaser(s)'s signature(s).

In addition to supplying the above information, you should do the following: (a) enclose the proper payment; (b) indicate on the outside of the envelope the following legend: "Tender for Treasury Notes (Bonds)," and (c) mail the letter to a Federal Reserve bank.

Treasury notes and bonds are sold at auction in the same manner as Treasury bills. Also, as in the case of bills, you should submit a noncompetitive bid for the notes and bonds. This, in effect, states that you agree to pay an average price of the competitive bids, as determined by the Treasury Department. The price of the note or bond may be above or below par. Above par, for example, would mean that the price of $1,000 face value note is set at an amount more than $1,000, and that you must send more money if your initial payment covered only the face value of the note. Below par would mean that the price of a $1,000 face value note is set at an amount less than that and that you will receive a check for the difference.

There are times when the payment for notes or bonds must include the principal amount of the securities and the accrued interest on the securities from the date of the last scheduled interest payment to the effective date of the purchase of the securities. Notice of this additional part of the payment usually appears on the front page of the tender in fairly bold type. The amount of this additional payment is always expressed as the amount per $1,000 of the securities purchased, for the precise period of time for which the interest has accrued. The amount of this accrued interest will be included in the next scheduled interest payment.

Interest Earnings

Treasury notes and bonds carry a fixed interest coupon rate. This enables you to determine the coupon interest rate quickly by applying this rate to the face value of the note or bond. The interest earnings are payable twice a year by the U.S. Treasury Department. Occasionally, under the terms of the official offering circular, the period from the date of issue to the first interest payment date may be more or less than six months. When this occurs, the first interest payment will be an amount larger or smaller than the remaining payments. All subsequent interest payments will be for a six-month period and will be one-half of the dollar amount to be paid annually under the terms of the offering.

When your notes or bonds mature, you will be notified by the U.S. Treasury Department. Treasury securities do not earn interest after their maturity date.

TREASURY DIRECT SYSTEM

Treasury Direct is the book-entry securities system for investors who elect to have their Treasury securities in book-entry accounts maintained on the records of the Treasury Department, Bureau of Public Debt. Securities held in Treasury Direct can be purchased at a Federal Reserve bank or branch, or at the Treasury. All Federal Reserve banks and their branches and the Bureau of Public Debt of the U.S. Treasury Departments are Treasury Direct servicing offices. At any of these offices, investors can purchase Treasury bills, notes, or bonds; transfer these securities from one account to another; or request detailed information on their accounts.

Treasury Direct book-entry accounts are designed primarily for investors who plan to retain their securities from issue to maturity. An investor can establish a single master account for all marketable Treasury securities purchased which are eligible to be maintained in Treasury Direct.

Statement of Account

Investors receive a Statement of Account after establishing an account in Treasury Direct, and whenever certain transactions occur within their account.

The statement of account is not only a copy of the Account Master Record, but also a portfolio of all the investor's holdings in marketable Treasury securities, including the price associated with each security in the portfolio. This document simplifies the investor's recordkeeping and offers built-in flexibility, since changes to the account can be made very quickly.

Treasury Direct will normally send the statement to the owner's correspondence address designated in the Account Master Record.

Whenever the statements are issued as a result of a change in ownership of a security, they will be sent, where appropriate, to both the former and current owners.

Other Options

In addition to establishing a single master account, Treasury Direct offers a broad choice of registration options that includes single ownership, joint ownership with right of survivorship, joint ownership without right of survivorship, and co-ownership.

Reinvestment

A request for reinvestment of Treasury bills for a period of up to two years may be made at the time of original purchase. A request for an extended reinvestment may be for any eligible term, but the term must remain constant throughout the two-year extended reinvestment period. Subsequent requests to reinvest Treasury bills or to cancel a previous reinvestment request must be received no later than twenty days prior to the maturity date to ensure processing.

Book-Entry

Investors in Treasury bills, notes, and bonds no longer receive engraved certificates as evidence of their holdings in government securities. Except for certain foreign targeted issues, these marketable Treasury securities are currently issued only in book-entry form. Book-entry securities are represented by accounting entries that are maintained electronically.

Securities held in the Treasury Direct book-entry account are paid at maturity, unless the purchaser has elected to reinvest the proceeds of the maturing securities in new securities. Reinvestments are made only on a noncompetitive basis.

Before securities maintained in the Treasury Direct system can be sold or pledged, they must first be transferred to the commercial book-entry system. A request for transfer must be received no later than twenty days before an interest payment date or the maturity date of the security.

With book-entry securities, interest and the par amount at

maturity are paid automatically, and do not require presentation of a certificate. Transactions are handled much more quickly and efficiently, and book-entry eliminates the risk of loss or theft associated with registered securities.

Direct Deposit

Direct deposit under the Treasury Direct system is the method used to pay investors by electronically crediting their accounts in qualified financial institutions. Regular payments of interest and principal under Treasury Direct are made by direct deposit. Checks are issued only in extraordinary circumstances, as determined by the Treasury.

Process for Payments. Direct deposit works through a nationwide electronic payments network to automatically deposit payments from the investor's Treasury holdings into an account that the investor designates at his or her financial institution. When an individual makes an initial purchase of Treasury securities, he or she will be asked to specify a checking, savings, or share draft account number at a financial institution into which payments from securities investments can be deposited. Once this is done, the Treasury Direct system will notify the financial institution that it will be receiving electronic payments of funds for deposit into the designated account. Each time a payment of principal or interest is due, it will be deposited directly into this account.

Establishing an Account. To establish direct deposit, an investor will be asked to designate:

1. the name of the financial institution to receive payment from investment of securities;
2. the name(s) on the account to receive direct deposit payments;
3. the account number to which the direct deposits should be made;
4. the financial institution's nine-digit American Banker's Association Routing Transit Number (found at the bottom of a check or deposit slip) or a similar type routing number (obtained by contacting the financial institution);
5. the type of account (checking or savings).

FORECASTING YIELDS ON TREASURY SECURITIES

Financial counselors are quick to point out one disadvantage of investing in Treasury securities sold at auction—the fact that the investor does not know, prior to making the investment, the yield or rate of interest the investment will pay. However, as was pointed out in chapter 2, careful reading of the newspaper, along with simple analysis, will enable you to do a reasonably good job of forecasting the yield on Treasury securities at upcoming auctions. For an idea on the direction that the yield on Treasury bills will take, the discussion in chapter 2 suggested that you review the money supply data announced by the Federal Reserve on Thursday afternoons and published in Fridays' newspapers, and look for any announcements on changes in the discount rate.

Another guide you should consult to forecast yields on Treasury notes and bonds is "Quotations on Government Securities" or "Treasury Issues," a table that appears in the financial section of most major newspapers. These tables will provide you with the most recent market yield for various issues of Treasury notes and bonds, yields that are not likely to change dramatically within twenty-four hours. If you are considering buying Treasury notes and bonds later in the day, the tables will give you an estimate of the yield that the auction is likely to produce.

To illustrate the value of the market quotations in forecasting yields, consider the announcement by the Treasury department on its plans to auction seven-year notes on January 5, 1987 in $1,000 minimum denominations. As a prospective investor you could have waited until the morning of January 5 and reviewed the quotations in the morning newspaper. Exhibit 10–2 is a clipping of these quotations from a morning newspaper, and it shows that yields on December 1989 and January 1990 notes were 7.87 and 7.95 percent respectively at the close of the previous day's market. If these particular yields, or something very close to them, had been acceptable to you, you would have had until 1:00 p.m. EST to enter the auction by submitting a tender and the $5,000 purchase price to a Federal Reserve bank (or branch or the Bureau of Public Debt). Exhibit 10–3 is an article from the next morning's newspaper. As you can see, the article announces that the yield on that three-year note was 7.94 percent, which was only seven and one basis points

NEW YORK (AP)—Over-the-Counter U.S.
Treasury Bonds and Notes for Monday.
Bid and asked prices in dollars and 32nds.
Subject to Federal taxes but not State income
taxes.

k — Non-U.S. citizen exempt from
withholding taxes. n — Treasury note.
p — Treasury note and non-U.S. citizen
exempt from withholding taxes.
Source — Bloomberg L.P.

Source: Richmond Times-Dispatch, June 26, 1987

Exhibit 10–3

Markets

● WASHINGTON — Yields on three-year Treasury notes rose to the highest level since early last year as the government held the first of three auctions this week to raise $28 billion.

The average yield was 7.94 percent, up from 7.91 percent at the last auction on May 5.

● MILAN, Italy — Prices tumbled on the Milan stock market for the seventh consecutive session, as the turnaround after two strong years picked up steam on Italy's biggest exchange.

The fall brought the Milan market index's loss for the first two days of the week to nearly 6 percent. The big selloff by domestic and foreign investors knocked the equivalent of $5.3 billion from the market's value.

Source: Richmond Times-Dispatch, June 27, 1987

(100 basis points equal one percent) below the two market quotations in the previous morning's newspaper.

STATE AND LOCAL BONDS

The debt instruments issued by state and local governments, referred to as municipals, include bonds issued by states, counties, cities, towns, villages, school districts, and all authorities and special districts created by states. A special group of municipals are bonds issued by a public housing authority. These are often called "housings".

Bonds issued by these governmental units are further classified on the basis of their backing. The bonds with the most secured backing are called general obligation bonds, for which the issuing governmental unit pledges its full faith, credit, and taxing power as security. In essence, these are bonds in which the governmental unit guarantees the payment of interest and return of principal through the taxes that it can legally levy on its constituency. The other main classification of municipals is called "revenue bonds". These are debts in which the issuing governmental unit pays the interest and principal to the investor with income derived from the project that the bonds financed. The projects are usually public facilities such as toll bridges, turnpikes, and dormitories at public colleges.

Tax Advantage

No doubt the main attraction of municipals as investments is the tax advantage for the investor. For example, interest earnings from all municipals are exempt from federal income taxes. If you live in a state that has an income tax, the interest earnings from all bonds issued by that state and its local governmental units are also exempt from the state income tax. Interest earnings from bonds issued by one state, however, are taxable by another state. Because of the tax advantage enjoyed by municipals, these bonds are often referred to as "tax-exempts".

Although the tax advantage of municipals should not be overlooked when you are searching for investments, you should not invest in these securities simply because the interest earnings are tax-exempt. You can calculate how much taxable interest it would take to match a given rate of tax-exempt interest by using the formula that follows. You need to know the marginal tax rates applied to your taxable income on federal, state, and local returns. If you don't know them, check the rate schedules on each return for the highest percentage rate at which your income is taxed. Remember to use taxable income in the formula, not gross income.

Include the state and local rates only for issues that are exempt from those levies as well as from federal tax. For example, if you have $30,000 of taxable income on a joint return, you have a marginal federal tax rate of 36 percent. The issue is exempt from state income tax, where your marginal rate is 5 percent, and there is no local income tax where you live. You want to know the taxable equivalent yield on a municipal bond paying 6 percent.

Convert each of the tax rates to decimals, then use the formula: equivalent taxable yield $= 6\%/1 - (36 + 0.5 + 0) = 6\%/.59 = 10.17\%$.

To get as much money as you would earn from this 6 percent tax-free bond, you'd have to find a taxable investment yielding better than 10 percent.

Safety

If your analysis of various investments indicate that you could gain most by investing in municipals, then you should give serious thought to buying general obligation bonds. The yield or rate of return on these bonds is lower than that of other bonds. However, general obligation bonds have a high degree of safety, which enables you to plan your financial future with the utmost confidence. The rating agencies evaluate municipals, taking into consideration such factors as the area's tax base, population, statistics, total debt outstanding, and general economic climate.

Because revenue bonds do not have the full taxing power of the governmental unit behind them, they ought to be scrutinized more closely as a potential investment. One of the problems in considering the purchase of these bonds is that it is difficult to generalize about the relative safety of various revenue bonds. Currently, for example, some revenue bonds issued for turnpikes are in arrears on the payment of interest. Other revenue bonds issued for turnpikes are selling at a premium. The yields on revenue bonds are annually very competitive, but you ought to weigh the yield against the risk. As a general proposition, households with modest resources should rarely invest in revenue bonds.

It may interest you to know that fewer than 1 percent of the municipal bonds issued since the Great Depression have gone into default. It is also important to note that about 77 percent of all municipal bond defaults have occurred in bonds issued to finance revenue producing enterprises, such as utilities, bridges, or nuclear power plants. Lower yielding general obligation bonds backed by the full faith credit and taxing authority of a state or local government or public agency are definitely the interest-bearing municipal bonds to buy.

Buying Individual Bonds

Although the face value of most municipals is either $5,000 or $10,000, your broker may occasionally find an issue with a face of $1,000. It is for this reason that most financial advisors suggest that investors with limited funds should buy municipals by way of investing in a municipal bond mutual fund or a unit trust investment trust. Both of these types of investments will be discussed in greater detail in the chapter on mutual funds.

If you are willing to engage in a limited amount of research and are inclined to scrutinize very closely all information on a particular bond issue, then the buying of individual bonds should be more cost efficient. This is particularly true if you do not plan to trade the bonds on a frequent basis. By buying individual bonds, your net return will be higher.

As a novice in investments, you should confine your purchase of municipals to insured or top-quality triple A–rated bonds. Although insured bonds usually offer a lower yield than uninsured bonds of similar quality, the peace of mind that the insurance brings is worth the price.

Housings

Most investors are not very familiar with bonds issued by public housing authorities. Because these bonds are issued by, and are the direct obligation of, local housing authorities or agencies, and becauses these authorities build public housing for low-income tenants, most investors view the bonds as straight revenue bonds. Some investors might think of public housing bonds as a very risky investment because they have a negative view of low-income families' sense of responsibility about paying rent. Public housing bonds, however, are not risky investments. Such bonds are issued under the provision of the Federal Housing Act of 1949. And although each issue is secured by a pledge of the net rental revenues of a local housing project, the Public Housing Administration agrees to make annual payments to the fiscal agent of each bond issue, in an amount sufficient to meet the estimated annual **debt service**, for a period of up to forty years, regardless of the physical or financial standing of the local housing project. This applies, however, only to multiple family public housing.

Thus, in effect, public housing bonds are backed by the federal government, and have the added advantage of being exempt from federal, state, and local income taxes (in the state where the authority is located). In addition to these advantages, public housing

---

• **debt service:** interest requirements plus stipulated payments of principal on outstanding debt.

bonds generally contain adequate **call protection** for investors, and they are often available in $1,000 denominations.

GOVERNMENT SECURITIES VS. OTHER INVESTMENTS

Nowadays when one compares an investment in government securities with an investment in other financial instruments, it is not enough to focus on such factors as safety, marketability, liquidity, and tax avoidance. Other financial instruments, such as consumer type CDs and money market CDs sold by banks and thrift institutions, are insured by an agency of the federal government, thereby providing the same degree of safety as a Treasury note or a Treasury bill. Also, the **secondary market** for corporate stocks and bonds is just as active as the one for Treasury securities, and a number of mutual funds invest only in municipal bonds, a factor that enables them to offer tax-exempt earnings to their investors. Thus, many of the attractive features once belonging only to government securities are now a part of many other financial instruments. This leaves the question, "Should you as an investor favor an investment in government securities over an investment in other financial instruments?"

As with many other questions, the best answer here would not be a categorical yes or no. The answer may well depend on such factors as:

1. how much money you have to invest;
2. whether your immediate objective is income or retirement security;
3. the amount of your current investments in assets other than financial instruments;
4. your tax bracket;

- **call protection:** the specific period of time during which a callable securities issue cannot be recalled.
- **secondary market:** a market for buying and selling previously issued securities.

5. the amount of time and effort you are willing to devote to monitoring your investments;

6. whether your state or city has an income tax;

7. your forecast of interest rates;

8. the particular kind of government securities and other financial instruments you are considering.

Let's consider a few typical sets of circumstances for you as an average wage earner with current income of less than $25,000 a year. If you have $1,000 to invest, and you need additional income to supplement your current budget, you should probably favor the purchase of a consumer-type CD at a commercial bank or thrift over the various government securities, because you can schedule the receipt of interest earnings monthly or quarterly, whereas the interest earnings from Treasury notes are payable only twice a year. In the same set of circumstances, as a single person in a fairly high tax bracket, you might be better off buying a general obligation municipal bond. This would not produce the extra income as frequently, but the net income for the year would be larger, because all of the interest earnings would be exempt from taxes. In a third set of circumstances, we can continue to assume that you have $1,000 to invest, that you want immediate income, and that you are in a fairly low tax bracket. This could persuade you to sacrifice the frequency of extra income and search for the highest interest rate available, which would probably be in corporate bonds. If there is a choice between a debenture bond from a top-rated firm and a secured bond from a medium-rated firm, you should go with the debenture even though it is not secured by any tangible collateral that is.

As an average wage earner with very modest resources available for investment, you should decide whether to invest in government securities or other financial instruments only after a careful analysis of the eight factors mentioned earlier. Above all, you should refrain from making decisions solely on the basis of a desire to diversify your investments. While there is some merit in **diversification** at certain stages in your economic life cycle, diversification alone

---

• **diversification:** spreading investments among different companies and institutions in different fields.

cannot assure the achievement of your financial goals. In making your investment choices, each decision should be based on one or more of the "Guidelines for Judging Investments" (in chapter 7). If this leads you to put all of your investments in government securities, or in nongovernment financial instruments, you are justified in limiting your flexibility in order to achieve one of your financial goals.

11 ·
Mutual
Funds

If you lack the time, knowledge, and energy to choose and manage your investments in securities, then you should consider placing your funds with an investment company. There are a variety of very reputable investment companies in the United States today. While these companies are not eligible for federal insurance, their history shows an outstanding record of safety, and their staffs are composed of highly competent managers. The typical investment company— whether organized in the form of a trust, partnership, organized group, or corporation—is engaged primarily in the business of investing in securities. Of the various kinds of investment companies, the four most prominent are **open-end**, **closed-end**, unit **investment trusts**, and issuers of **variable annuities**. Most of the discussion in this chapter will focus on open-end investment companies, usually referred to as mutual funds. There will be some references, however, to closed-end investment companies and unit investment trusts.

- **open-end:** companies in which new shares of the fund are sold whenever there is a request.
- **closed-end:** companies in which there is a set number of shares to be sold, and are outstanding. The shares are traded on the major exchanges.
- **investment trusts:** any firm that takes its capital and invests it in other companies.
- **variable annuity:** an annuity contract providing lifetime retirement payments that vary in amount with the results of investment in a separate account portfolio.

A mutual fund is an open-end investment company, with a managed portfolio of securities that will buy back shares from investors whenever the investor wishes to sell. The redemption price depends upon the value of the company's portfolio at that time. There is no secondary trading market for the shares of such companies. There is also the closed-end investment company which, unlike a mutual fund, does not continuously offer to buy back its shares at the options of its shareholders. After the sale of shares by a closed-end investment company, the shares are traded in the **secondary market** like the shares of any other public corporation. Still another type of investment company is a unit investment trust. The portfolio of a unit investment trust is fixed and not actively managed. However, as with mutual funds, interests in a unit investment trust are redeemable at their net asset value at the option of their holders.

A mutual fund is referred to as a load fund when the selling price of its shares includes a sale charge. Shares of such companies may be purchased through broker/dealers who receive part of the sales charge. By the same token, the mutual fund is known as a no-load fund if the selling price of its shares does not contain a sales charge. Shares of a no-load mutual fund may be purchased directly from the investment.

There are other ways in which mutual funds are classified. The most popular types of classifications are based on the kind of securities that the fund manages. Such classifications include stock (or equity) funds, tax-free (or tax-exempt) funds, and balanced (stocks and bonds) funds. Within these classifications, an investor can choose an **aggressive growth stock fund** or an **income stock fund**; a low-grade corporate bond fund or a high-grade corporate bond fund.

- **secondary market:** a market for buying and selling previously issued securities.
- **aggressive growth stock fund:** a mutual fund in which the portfolio of securities consists mostly of stocks that are expected to appreciate in value in the very near future.
- **income stock fund:** a mutual fund in which the portfolio consists mostly of stocks noted for producing generous dividends.

CHOOSING A FUND

For the new and inexperienced investor, choosing a mutual fund for investment makes a lot of sense. First, the investor saves a great deal of time that would be expended on research if he or she decided to buy individual securities through a dealer. Second, for a very small fee, the investor gets the expertise of professional managers. Third, the investor gets diversification, which is usually recommended for any investment portfolio.

Goals of the Investor

As a first step in investing in mutual funds, you should always review your specific financial goals. Remember, financial goals vary greatly. Remember too that no single mutual fund can fit the needs of all investors, or even the changing needs of one investor. A young investor may be more interested in securities with growth potential, while an older investor may be more interested in increasing his or her current income, and an even older investor may be more concerned with avoiding risk.

Another factor that you should consider before selecting a mutual fund is whether the fund is a member of a **family of funds**. A family of funds is an investment company that manages a growth fund, an income fund, a balanced fund, and many others, and gives the investor the privilege of exchanging shares from one fund to another. The exchange privilege is an advantage when the investor's objectives and goals change. For example, a young couple may be interested in a growth fund during early years, but may need more current income after they have children. This latter development should prompt an exchange of shares held in a growth fund for shares in an income fund. Thus, a family of funds allows investors to change the focus of their investment strategy quickly and efficiently, thereby saving time and money.

You should understand that investment companies are non-

- **family of funds:** a number of mutual funds managed by the same investment company, with each fund specializing in a different kind of security or investment product.

depository institutions, and your invested money is not insured by a federal agency. Many of these companies, however, have an excellent record of safety.

Making the Purchase

Many mutual funds are advertised in the financial section of most daily newspapers. You may also request from your local banker the names and addresses of selected funds that the bank is familiar with or that have accounts at the bank. Upon request, most investment companies that offer mutual funds will send you a prospectus that describes their operation and how you buy mutual fund shares.

Although all mutual funds share common features, many have individual characteristics that appeal to investors with different tastes. For example, a fund that invests primarily in Treasury bills may appeal more to very conservative investors than would those funds that invest primarily in commercial paper or CDs of foreign banks. Thus, before deciding to invest in a particular fund, you should examine its prospectus carefully with respect to the fund's investments. If you are not confident in your ability to evaluate a fund's investments, you should consult one of the rating services. An example of such a service is the Institute for Econometric Research, which publishes Money Fund Safety Ratings. This publication uses a letter rating system similar to that for bonds (AAA, AA, A, BB, etc.), and the ratings are based on quality of assets, diversification, average portfolio maturity, and **volatility**.

After very carefully reviewing the prospectuses from a number of funds and then choosing a fund, you should:

1. complete the purchase application furnished with the prospectus;
2. make a check or money order to the fund in the amount stipulated as the minimum investment;
3. send the check or money order and the purchase application to the fund at the address stipulated in the prospectus.

• **volatility:** a measure of the rapidity with which a security changes in value as compared with the market generally.

Accounts opened in more than one name will be registered as joint tenants with rights of survivorship, unless indicated otherwise. When registering these accounts, the signatures of all joint tenants are required on redemption-by-mail and change-of-registration requests.

Remember, when you buy shares in a mutual fund, you are actually buying ownership interests or common stock in the fund. Usually there is no charge or fee for the purchase, and the minimum investment might be as low as $500. Each fund's prospectus describes the procedure for purchasing shares; however, all funds will accept purchases upon receipt of payment and a completed application. Many funds will accept initial subscriptions by telephone.

Generally, additional minimum investments range from $100 to $1,000. Many funds will accept such additions by telephone, and some funds will even arrange for additional investments to be made through payroll deduction or from automatic monthly bank drafts drawn against the shareholder's checking account.

Safety

When considering a mutual fund as an investment, remember that your funds will not be insured by an agency of the federal government. However, mutual funds are required by the Securities and Exchange Commission to carry insurance against embezzlement, and many carry private insurance against other potential problems. Experience to date indicates that all mutual funds are being run on a sound basis, and that there is minimal risk to you as an investor because of the short-term nature and type of the fund's investments.

MONEY MARKET MUTUAL FUNDS

A money market instrument is a document that accommodates borrowing and lending for periods of one year or less. The rate of interest involved supposedly reflects the true relationship between the current supply of and demand for loanable funds. Typically, these short-term instruments consist of domestic commercial bank certificates of deposit, U.S. Treasury bills, and high-grade

Table 11–1. COMPOSITION OF MMMF ASSETS (June 1986, in Billions)

	Amount	*% of Total*
U.S. Treasury bills	15.4	6.9
Other Treasury securities	6.9	3.1
Other U.S. securities	14.8	6.7
Repurchase agreements	32.2	14.5
Commercial bank CD[1]	12.7	5.7
Other Domestic CD[2]	4.2	1.9
Eurodollar CD[3]	22.1	10.0
Commercial Paper	98.6	44.4
Bankers' acceptances	10.9	4.9
Other	4.3	1.9
Total assets	222.0	100.0

[1] Commercial bank CDs are those issued by American banks located in the United States.
[2] Other domestic CDs include those issued by S&Ls and American branches of foreign banks.
[3] Eurodollar CDs are those issued by foreign branches of domestic banks and some issued by Canadian banks; this category includes some one-day paper.

Source: Investment Company Institute.

commercial paper. Other short-term instruments might consist of **banker's acceptances, Eurodollar** certificates of deposit, **repurchase agreements**, and various other U.S. agency issues. (See table 11–1.) Although it takes at least $100,000 to purchase most

- **commercial paper:** short-term, unsecured promissory notes (IOUs) issued by well-known and well-regulated business firms.
- **banker's acceptances:** future claims on a bank backed by the bank's customer; they enable the bank to finance the customer's business transactions, such as a shipment of goods by a third party.
- **Eurodollar:** deposits denominated in U.S. dollars at banks and other financial institutions outside the United States.
- **repurchase agreements:** agreements by a bank or the Federal Reserve to buy back, under certain terms, securities that it originally sold to a second party.

money market instruments, small savers can make money market investments by buying shares in a money market mutual fund (MMMF). As a shareholder, your earnings are dividends distributed from the profits made by the company. In making your decision to invest in a MMMF, note that the fund offers the following:

1. higher interest rates or earnings than some of the traditional investments, particularly passbook savings accounts;

2. no commissions or fees charged when you buy or redeem your MMMF shares, as against commissions charged when you buy stocks and bonds through brokers;

3. easy access to your money on request without penalty, as against the penalty for liquidating a consumer-type CD before maturity;

4. limited check-writing privileges to third parties;

5. reasonably low minimum deposits and required maintenance balances;

6. flexibility in increasing your investment;

7. a monthly statement showing your earnings for the month, as well as all transactions involving your account during the month.

Checkwriting and Withdrawals

Most MMMFs have an option that allows shareholders to write checks. In some cases, a minimum amount for each check is stipulated, although competition is gradually causing this stipulation to be dropped. When you write a check on an MMMF, you are both withdrawing funds and redeeming some of your shares. Your check to a third party is drawn from an account that the MMMF has at a commercial bank. When the check is presented for payment, the bank, as agent for you as a shareholder, cashes in enough of your shares to cover the check, depositing the money in the MMMFs account with the bank. This allows you to continue to earn dividends on your funds while the check is being cleared.

In addition to writing checks, you can, of course, withdraw funds simply by requesting a return of some of your shares. In effect, you would be redeeming some of your shares, and you can do this by the phone or by wire request, in which case your money would be either mailed or wired to your bank account. Also, you can close your entire account or redeem all of your shares whenever you wish. It is possible, however, that the redemption value of your shares may be more or less than the amounts you have invested, depending on the market value of your shares at the time of redemption. Each fund's prospectus should be consulted for the specific redemption procedures required by the fund.

Your Earnings

In its prospectus, an MMMF quotes a yield on the potential shareholder's investment. This yield, however, reflects the prior experience of the MMMF, and is actually intended only as an indication of the possible yield. MMMF managers cannot guarantee the future yield on MMMF shares because the yields on **money market assets** vary over time, and because the yield on MMMF shares reflects the level and variability of the yields of the underlying money market assets. Experience shows that the yield for MMMF's tend to trail market rate trends. Thus, when short-term market rates are rising, MMMF yields will lag behind; when short-term market rates are declining, MMMF yields will fall later.

Yields

In quoting their yields, just about all MMMFs use a seven-day yield, which may be found in your local newspaper, as shown in exhibit 11–1. However, yields on these funds are reported in three ways: seven-day average yield; thirty-day average yield, and twelve-month average yield. All three are expressed in terms of an average annualized yield. The following is a brief explanation of these three yields:

- *The seven-day yield* is what the fund would pay over the course of a year if it continued to earn exactly what it earned over the preceding seven days. Because the seven-day average yield measures the most recent performance of money funds, it's the best yield to look at when trying to determine the direction of interest rates.

- **money market assets:** investments in financial instruments, such as bank certificates of deposit and short-term Treasury securities.

Exhibit 11-1

MONEY MARKET FUNDS

NEW YORK (AP) — The following quotations, collected by the NASD Inc. are the average of annualized yields and dollar-weighted portfolio maturities for the seven-day period ending Friday, Dec. 11. Yield based upon actual dividends paid (total return) to shareholders.

MONEY MARKET:	Days	Yield	Chs.

Source: Richmond Times-Dispatch, Sunday, July 12, 1987

• *The thirty-day yield* is what the fund would pay over the course of a year if it continued to earn exactly what it earned over the preceding thirty days.
• *The twelve-month yield* shows what the fund actually paid on average over the past year. Use the twelve-month yield when making historical comparisons, such as comparing how you did in the stock market last year with how well you would have done if your money had been in a money fund.

To arrive at the seven-day yield, the fund first adds the average daily interest accrued to the average daily discount earned per share on the fund's portfolio for that seven-day period, exclusive of gains or losses on portfolio instruments. The fund then subtracts the average daily provision for expenses per share for the seven-day period. This sum, the average daily net income per share, is then multiplied by 365. The result is the fund's average net yield for that seven-day period stated as though it were an annual yield.

The following illustrates the yield calculation for an MMMF for the seven-day period ending April 11, 1987:

Average daily interest accrued (net of premium amortization)
    and average daily discount earned (including original issue
    and market discount) per share . . . . $.0004096
Less average daily provision for expenses per share . . . . (.000318)
    Average daily net income per share . . . . $.0003778
Annualized average net yield (average daily net income per
    share divided by the average daily net asset value per share of
    $1.00 × 365 . . . . 13.79%

The earnings from your investment in a MMMF are dividends, and these dividends are generated from interest payments on the various money market instruments after the fund's expenses are deducted. Dividends are usually declared daily, and you may elect to receive these as cash on a regular monthly or quarterly basis or you may have them reinvested in additional shares. Most, if not all, MMMFs provide monthly detailed account statements to their shareholders.

Expected Results

Although a fund's past performance cannot guarantee the same results, it can prove useful to look at the five-year pattern of results shown by the fund you are considering. This record should allow you to determine how well a fund performs under varying economic environments.

Above all you should not be persuaded to invest in the latest "hot" fund, because in many instances, last year's spectacular performer will likely be this year's "bust." Remember, you should not be trying to get rich overnight. Rather, you should be aiming for a consistently reasonable return on your investment with funds inside families of funds that meet your personal investment criteria.

TAX-EXEMPT FUNDS

Tax-exempt funds invest in securities issued by state and local government entities. These funds are so named because they pay interest income that is exempt from federal income taxes. A small number of tax-exempt funds buy only the securities issued by governments within a particular state, such as California, Massachusetts, or New York. These funds offer investors from those states interest income that is exempt from both federal and state—and sometimes local—income taxes.

Tax-exempt funds are sometimes referred to as municipal bond funds, or just plain "bond funds." There are two types of these funds. By far the most popular type, in terms of investor participation, is the open-end mutual fund.

For persons contemplating their first investment into the municipals market, the best way to get started is with a tax-exempt mutual fund. These funds buy and sell municipal bonds in response to changing interest rate and credit conditions. Investment in these funds is recommended for persons with $5,000 or less to invest, because the buy-in price on many funds is as little as $1,000, and additional shares can be purchased for $100 each.

If you are shopping for a bond fund, you should focus on the figure that indicates the total return. This figure combines interest from bonds and profits from bond trading and **options** selling with the change in market value of the bonds. Another factor to keep in mind while shopping for a bond fund is the management fee. These fees usually range from 0.50 percent to 1.5 percent of your assets in the fund each year. Naturally, you should seek the fund with the lowest management fee.

Tax-exempt mutual funds are appropriate for investors who plan to sell their holdings, perhaps when their children reach college age. Individual bonds, by contrast, are often difficult to unload. Brokers often charge as much as $20 for every $1,000 of bonds sold in trades of less than $25,000. Perhaps it should also be said that while tax-exempt mutual funds simplify the selection process of municipal bonds and spread the investment risk over a diversified portfolio of such bonds, the yields on the funds are often one-half to one full percentage point lower than those on individual bonds.

UNIT INVESTMENT TRUSTS

The portfolio of a unit investment trust (UIT) is fixed and not actively managed. However, as with mutual funds, interests in a unit investment trust are redeemable at their net asset value at the option of their holders. In addition, there is often a secondary trading market for the shares of UITs.

These trusts typically invest their assets in debt securities. Units in a trust are often sold to the public in $1,000 denominations. Distributions of interest may be made on a monthly, quarterly, semiannual, or annual basis. Some UITs may offer automatic reinvestment of interest, either in the trust or in a mutual fund run by the same sponsor.

In contrast to the tax-exempt mutual funds, UITs offer fixed portfolios of securities that rarely change, even if interest rates increase—unless a particular bond issue runs into trouble. Recent trends show that UITs feature yields about one percentage point

---

• **option:** the right to buy or sell something at a specified price within a specified time period.

higher than those offered by municipal bond mutual funds. Moreover, the risk of losing the principal of your investment because of rising rates is lower, because UITs have fixed portfolios. You can simply hold your shares until maturity, when the bonds are paid off at face value. Because mutual fund portfolios are constantly changing, they do not have a fixed maturity and it is more difficult to avoid interest-rate risk. On the other hand, UITs cannot take advantage of quick changes in the marketplace, as can mutual funds.

Just as there are tax-exempt mutual funds, there are also tax-exempt unit trusts. These trusts are diversified portfolios of municipal bonds that are sold to the public in units typically priced at about $1,000 or $5,000 each. Returns on these unit trusts are generally about one-quarter to one percentage point higher than those offered by municipal bond mutual funds. On the other hand, they have annual fees and upfront sales charges as high as 5 percent, which makes returns slightly lower than the returns on individually purchased municipal bonds.

If you decide to invest in tax-exempt unit trusts, try to find some way of evaluating the quality of the bonds in the trust's portfolio. You might find some information on the bonds in the trust's prospectus. Your objective should be a portfolio with bonds that have "investment grade" ratings—"BAA" or higher at Moody's Investors Service Inc. and "BBB" or higher at Standard & Poor's Corporation.

About one-half of the tax-exempt unit trusts now in operation carry some form of insurance to protect bondholders against default. Insurance usually gives a trust a triple-A credit rating, but it can also reduce an investor's returns by thirty to forty basis points. (One basis point is one one-hundredth of a percentage point).

INVESTMENT COMPANY PROSPECTUSES

If you are considering an investment in an open-end investment company or a unit investment trust, you should obtain and read a current prospectus before looking at other sales literature. Do not hesitate to seek advice if there is anything in the prospectus you do not understand. And if you do buy shares in the company, save the prospectus to refer to in the future. Among other things, the prospectus will tell you:

1. the company's investment objectives—in other words, whether it is designed to provide income, protect capital, minimize taxes, etc.;
2. the amount of any sales charges and the procedures for redeeming shares;
3. what risks may be involved in placing your money in that particular company.

CLOSED-END INVESTMENT COMPANIES

Unlike a mutual fund, a closed-end investment company does not continuously offer to buy back its shares at the option of its shareholders. Such a company also does not continuously offer to sell its shares. After an initial sale by the company, the shares are traded in the secondary market like the shares of any other public corporation. Their price may fluctuate in response to changes in the value of a company's portfolio, as well as in response to the supply of and demand for its shares. When shares of such companies are traded with the services of a broker, it is customary for a commission to be charged.

"GINNIE MAE" FUNDS: MUTUAL FUNDS AND TRUSTS

Because of the high minimum of $25,000 for individual Ginnie Mae certificates, there are now Ginnie Mae mutual funds and Ginnie Mae unit trusts. The structure and management of these funds is similar to that of the tax-exempt funds. The purchase price of shares and units ranges from $1,000 to $5,000. Ginnie Mae mutual funds are actively managed, while a Ginnie Mae unit trust is a fixed basket of securities, far more sensitive to market risks.

For both the mutual funds and the unit trusts, the underlying mortgages for the shares and units are insured by the Federal Housing Administration or guaranteed by the Veterans Administration or the Farmers Home Administration. This means that the federal government guarantees only the scheduled payments from the underlying Ginnie Mae certificates. It does not mean that the federal government guarantees the yield on Ginnie Mae funds.

If you are willing to read the prospectus thoroughly, then a

Ginnie Mae fund could be a good investment for your portfolio. These funds are devoid of any credit risk, and the Ginnie Mae certificate usually offers a fairly good yield. With a Ginnie Mae fund, you do not have to concern yourself with the complexity of prepayments and the bookkeeping usually required to separate the interest earnings from the payment of principal. Also, while a Ginnie Mae fund cannot prevent prepayments on mortgages and fluctuating yields, the diverse portfolio helps to offset these two factors.

TAX-EXEMPTS VS. TAXABLES
AND A BALANCED APPROACH

While tax-exempt funds have obvious advantages for some investors, such advantages are far from being universal. For example, individuals in a low tax bracket might well find that the return on a taxable investment would provide a higher overall yield. Also, since the Tax Reform Act of 1986 lowered the maximum marginal tax rate to 28 percent, compared with the previous maximum of 50 percent, even persons in the high income brackets need to compute the yields on both the tax-exempt and taxable investments before making a decision.

As a general proposition, an investor's decision as to whether to purchase a tax-exempt or taxable security depends largely on his or her marginal tax rate and the rates being paid on the tax-exempts and taxables.

The diversity of mutual funds and unit investment trusts allows you to create an investment strategy similar to those employed by professional investment managers. Their experience shows that one of the best approaches to managing money is to have a "balanced" approach. In effect, this approach means that you should not invest totally in stocks or totally in bonds, but to have over a period of time a mixture of both. The multitude of funds allows you to do just that. Your age and your household's stage in the life cycle should ultimately determine the allocation between various kinds of fund investments.

For guidance, a broadly based stock or equity fund could make up 45 percent of your portfolio of funds, while a good tax-exempt bond fund would comprise another 45 percent of the portfolio. The remaining 10 percent could be held in a money market fund until you decide to increase your position in either the stock fund or the municipal bond fund. This kind of strategy should lead to increasing returns for your portfolio and also to greater appreciation and understanding of the investment process.

12·
Retirement: Planning And Financing

According to figures released by the Metropolitan Life Insurance Company on June 27, 1987, Americans' life expectancy had reached 75 years. This gain came after two years in which average life expectancy had remained steady at 74.7 years. The expected life span was even greater for those who were older. Women who reached the age of 65 in 1986 had an average of 18.9 more years to live, and men 14.7 years.

The aforementioned data clearly show that the average age of Americans is increasing, and is expected to continue to increase up through the year 2020. Further, the data show that those persons who are fortunate enough to reach age sixty-five can count on living many more years. When these facts are coupled with surveys showing that many people are retiring at age sixty-two or at sixty-five, the necessity of financing one's retirement should come through loud and clear.

Prior to the life expectancy data released by the Metropolitan Life Insurance Company, the findings in a study conducted by Louis Harris & Associates among middle-aged workers left little doubt that pension plans and retirement income were among the major concerns of the average worker. They were fearful that inflation would reduce the purchasing power of their pensions and retirement benefits, and that they would not have sufficient income from other sources to maintain an acceptable standard of living.

These middle-aged workers advised younger workers to develop financial plans for retirement early in their careers and to manage their financial resources with a view toward supplementing their pensions and Social Security benefits. It was assumed that these financial plans would include any opportunities to contribute to a supplemental retirement program sponsored by an employer if such contributions would assure an increase in retirement income.

Needless to say, the aforementioned suggestions from those middle-aged workers is sound advice. All active workers today face important decisions about their economic life after retirement. While Social Security and regular pensions will no doubt constitute the major part of their retirement income, it should be clear to all of us that additional financial resources will mean the difference between a comfortable retirement and a level of living barely above the poverty line.

Until recently, the prevailing opinion was that the additional financial resources needed during retirement would come from being frugal and having enough self-discipline to "defer current gratification" for later comfort. Experience has shown, however, that this is only part of the task. Also necessary is a definite plan or strategy to guide the results of this frugality in a manner that will produce not only additional financial resources, but also growth of these resources sufficient to meet future changes in the economic environment.

Although it is never too soon to start planning for retirement, most wage-earners are in a better position to save and consider sizeable investments after their children are grown up and the mortgage consumes a smaller portion of their total income. Also, at this stage most wage earners are much more knowledgeable about investments and have more time to investigate and analyze their choices for investments.

There are a number of strategies you can pursue in developing your financial plans for retirement and selecting the best vehicles to achieve the objectives specified by these plans. This chapter will focus on a set of simplified plans that calls for analyzing all of the retirement programs offered by your employer that could affect your retirement income, and managing your current income with a view toward providing a measure of independent income during your retirement. As a starting point for these plans, you might want to develop a statement similar to the one shown below, and update it periodically until the date your retirement actually arrives.

MONTHLY OPERATING STATEMENT
IN RETIREMENT

Income	*Expenses*
Social Security	Medical
Pension	Church & charitable contributions
Earnings from investments	Real estate taxes
IRA	Vacations
Deferral Compensation Plan	Food, clothing, etc.

INVESTMENTS IN FINANCIAL INSTRUMENTS

In previous chapters on stocks, bonds, government securities, and mutual funds, you learned that there are various categories within each of these types of securities. You also learned that your selection of an investment in each category should depend on your financial and economic objectives. This advice should certainly be followed when your objective is to supplement your retirement income, and it is obvious that the best way of supplementing your retirement from investment is to select a category of securities for its ability to produce income.

Stocks

When the desire for income is the financial objective, you ought to give priority to two categories of stock. One category is preferred stock. As you recall from the chapter on stocks, preferred stock carries a fixed rate of dividends; holders of such stock receive their dividends before dividends are distributed to holders of common stock. If the corporation fails to pay the stipulated dividends to holders of preferred stock, the dividends accumulate and the total must be paid before any dividends can be distributed to holders of common stock. Thus preferred stock provides at least two of the factors that are essential to retirement income. One is stability, which means that the dividends are likely to be forthcoming as long as the corporation makes a profit—and sometimes even when the corporation does not make a profit. The other is the assured level of income, which facilitates planning for the income received during retirement.

Among the best stocks for achieving the aforementioned objectives are preferred and common stocks of utility companies, particularly electric utility companies. Most electric utilities are serving growing geographical areas, and the regional Bell companies now offer good yields and potential growth in earnings and dividends. This recommendation is bolstered by the findings in a recent study by the Edison Electric Institute, which concluded that "electric utility companies were both less risky and a more profitable investment vehicle for common stockholders than the average non-regulated corporations over the last 15 years."

Bonds

Bonds are commonly known as "fixed-income" securities, and retirees are often referred to as persons on "fixed-income." Both of these references are fairly accurate, and consequently suggest a logical match-up. The interest received on a bond will remain the same throughout the life of the bond, and it is assumed that the financial requirements of a retiree will not change materially during his or her lifetime. Although these assumptions are basically true, there are some exceptions, particularly in the components of the retiree's financial requirements.

With the aforementioned factors in mind, you should purchase bonds that will provide you with maximum interest earnings for an extended period of time. These objectives should not be difficult to achieve because bonds with longer maturities usually carry higher coupons or rates of interest. Also, because retired persons are usually in a lower tax bracket than they were before their retirement, they can seek those bonds with the highest rates without considering the tax equivalency.

To follow through on this part of your financial plan, you should favor the purchase of long-term Treasury bonds. Although the interest earnings on these bonds are subject to federal income taxes, the highest marginal tax rate is 28 percent, and the interest earnings are exempt from state and local income taxes. If you purchase these bonds directly from a Federal Reserve bank, one of its branches, or the Bureau of the Public Debt in Washington, D.C., you will not be required to pay any type of service fee. Also, you may make these purchases by mail if you follow the proper procedure. The offering schedule for all Treasury bonds is shown in exhibit 10–2.

TAX SHELTERS

Indeed, one of your strategies for supplementing your pension and Social Security benefits should consist of investing in one or more tax shelters. Basically, tax shelters are arrangements in which you are able to reduce your current tax liability in order to produce greater after-tax income during the later period. There are a variety of tax shelters. However, the category we will concentrate on in this discussion may be best described as a plan for tax-favored retirement savings. In essence, this plan involves tax-deferral and is designed to shift part of the taxpayer's income from a currently higher rate of taxation to a later period in the taxpayer's life, when his or her income is expected to be lower, and thus likely to be taxed at a lower rate. For most taxpayers and average wage earners, this later period is after retirement.

INDIVIDUAL RETIREMENT ACCOUNTS (IRAs)

Despite changes made in the Tax Reform Act of 1986, the Individual Retirement Account (IRA) continues to be a powerful retirement savings and investment vehicle. Anyone who earns income can still contribute up to $2,000 per year to an IRA account and earn tax-deferred interest on his or her money. Tax-deductible contributions to IRAs are still availble to individuals with incomes up to $25,000, to married couples with combined incomes up to $40,000, and to those at any income level not covered by employer-provided pension plans, including 401 (K) plans. If one spouse is covered by a plan, the other spouse is not eligible for a full IRA tax deduction on a joint tax return. Taxpayers ineligible to make tax-deductible contributions can continue to add to IRAs, although the contributions will be taxable. The interest earned by IRAs held by all taxpayers, including those ineligible for tax-deductible contributions, will continue to be tax-deferred.

Deduction Rules

To determine your status under a retirement or profit-sharing plan, you should consult your supervisor at work or the personnel department.

If you are not covered by an employer-provided pension plan, then you can continue to deduct from your gross income the full amount of your IRA contributions each year.

If you or your spouse is covered by such an employer-provided pension plan, the deductibility of your IRA contribution is determined according to your Adjusted Gross Income (AGI) as follows:

1. Single taxpayers making less than $25,000 a year can still claim the full amount of their IRA contribution up to $2,000 as a deduction.

2. Single taxpayers making between $25,000 and $35,000 can deduct their IRA contribution up to an amount that is defined as $2,000 minus $200 for each incremental $1,000 of AGI over $25,000. For example, if you make $26,000, you can contribute $2,000 to your IRA and $1,800 will be deductible, or you can contribute $1,800 and all of it will be deductible.

3. If the single taxpayer's income is greater than $35,000, his or her contributions to an IRA will not be deductible at all.

4. Married couples filing jointly who make a combined AGI of less than $40,000 can continue to take a full deduction for their IRA contributions. If only one spouse works, the combined contribution cannot exceed $2,250. If both work the combined contribution cannot exceed $4,000.

5. Married couples filing jointly can take a partial deduction if their combined income ranges between $40,000 and $50,000. The deductible contribution amount is again reduced $200 for each incremental $1,000 of AGI over $40,000.

6. Married couples filing jointly with combined AGIs of more than $50,000 will not be able to take a tax deduction for their IRA contribution.

7. Married couples filing separate returns face individual limitations. Contributions by a spouse who is *not* eligible or covered by a company retirement plan are deductible.

For contributions by a spouse who is covered or eligible for a retirement plan, deductibility is phased out between AGIs of $0 and $10,000. As above, the deductible amount is reduced $200 for each incremental $1,000 of AGI.

Investment Choices

You can open an IRA at commercial banks, savings institutions, brokerage firms, insurance companies, and mutual funds; or your employer may offer such an account in connection with a pension, profit-sharing, or savings plan.

You can put your IRA money into savings certificates, insurance company annuities, or Treasury certificates. You can take some additional risk and invest in mutual funds or stocks, in anticipation that the combination of dividends and capital gains will produce a higher return than guaranteed and federally insured investments. Because all IRA earnings are treated alike when they are eligible to be withdrawn, it may not be advisable to invest your IRA funds in municipal bonds because they usually carry lower interest rates. With very low tax liability during retirement, you should seek high-yield investments rather than low-yield investments that are tax-free.

Some financial institutions are advertising federally insured IRAs, along with the claim that your IRA will be worth over a million dollars at age sixty-five if you maintain a $2,000 yearly contribution from ages twenty-two to sixty-five. This sounds terrific, but you should examine this claim closely before establishing an IRA on this premise. First, can you be assured of receiving a specific yield on your IRA funds from the present time to the year in which you will reach age 65? Second, remember that the FDIC and FSLIC insure deposits only up to $100,000. Are you willing to go through the hassle of establishing IRAs at ten different financial institutions in order to have all of your IRA funds insured by an agency of the federal government?

You may prefer an account that invests in common stocks or long-term fixed rate bonds. You may buy U.S. Individual Retirement Bonds or U.S. Retirement Plan Bonds offered by the Treasury (purchase directly from a Federal Reserve bank or have a bank forward your application).

It is no longer permissible for institutions to invest your money in gold, gems, art, antiques, or other "collectibles."

Roll-Overs

Should you decide another IRA is more desirable than the one you have, you may transfer (roll-over) your investment from one plan to another, tax-free. All of the cash or other assets withdrawn must be put into the second account within sixty days. You may roll-over your IRA funds once a year, but not sooner than a year after any previous roll-over. For detailed rules, be sure to consult the Internal Revenue Service (IRS).

Withdrawals

You *may* begin withdrawing the money in your retirement account without penalty at age 59½ or if you become disabled. You *must* begin withdrawing before the end of the year in which you reach age 70½. Withdrawal may be in a lump sum or on a monthly, quarterly, or annual basis. Your withdrawals are considered to be income and, as such, are subject to income tax. But you will probably be in a lower tax bracket at the time.

Premature distribution (before age 59½) is subject to income tax and a 10% penalty tax. Additional penalties may also be incurred, such as the mandatory penalty for early withdrawal of certificates of deposit.

Note, too, that a financial institution *may* elect to impose an early withdrawal penalty, even after age 59½, if any funds withdrawn are part of a time deposit not yet matured.

IRA and IRS

IRAs remain a valuable long-term investment vehicle, allowing you to put money aside for your retirement and earn income on that money. (There are still penalties for early withdrawals, of course, so it doesn't pay to regard your IRA as a short-term savings plan.) The earnings and interest on your IRA investments won't be taxed until withdrawals begin—and the benefit of such tax-deferred earnings, especially over a long period, can be considerable.

The Internal Revenue Service (IRS) offers a publication on how to calculate deductions for IRAs, prorated spousal IRAs, and prorated IRAs for married people filing separately. The IRS publication also explains the complicated rules for withdrawal of deductible and nondeductible contributions. Workers who claim contributions to an IRA must file IRS Form 8606 when filing their federal income tax.

401 (K) PLANS

Let's hope that you are fortunate enough to work for an employer that offers its employees the opportunity to participate in a 401 (K) plan. Most financial analysts agree that this is one of the most valuable employee benefits an employer can offer. It is a plan in which you can supplement your traditional retirement income with earnings from an investment that consists of not only your accumulated savings but matching funds from your employer as well.

The term 401 (K) refers to a specific section of the Internal Revenue Code, authorizing a unique type of employee benefit plan that permits employees to elect to defer current taxation on a portion of their salary contributed to a qualified plan. The plan is indeed unique in the sense that it offers employees the opportunity to forego spending a portion of their salary in order to invest in their future financial security—with assistance through employer matching contributions on behalf of employees. This plan is often referred to as a cash or deferred arrangement and a salary-reduction plan; however, it is most commonly known as the Deferred Compensation option. In addition to providing you with supplemental retirement income, this plan can serve other financial needs as well—through payouts at termination of employment or death and through certain types of withdrawals and loans permitted during your active career.

How the Plan Works

Under the Deferred Compensation plan, your contributions are deducted from your salary before current federal income taxes (and, in most states, state income taxes) are withheld. Your employer matches this portion of your salary based on its own formula. Some formulas call for a match of fifty cents on a dollar. A few employers put in as much as two dollars for each dollar contributed by an employee. The combined funds are then invested in any one or several of a wide range of assets or funds, with the opportunity for you to change investments on a fairly frequent basis. In many cases, the employer places the funds in a guaranteed investment contract from an insurance company (similar to a CD but backed by the insurance company, not federal deposit insurance). There is a 10 percent penalty on early withdrawal of funds from a 401 (K) plan investment before age 59½, unless the withdrawal is related to health, disability, hardship or certain eligible medical expenses.

When you begin to make withdrawals from your 401 (K) plan account after you reach age 59½, you will have to pay taxes on these amounts, which will consist of your previous contributions, capital gains, interest, and dividends. However, in many instances, these withdrawals will be at a time when your marginal tax rate is lower than during your active career.

Your Contribution

When you enroll in the plan, you will be asked to indicate the percentage of your salary you wish to contribute to the plan. The maximum amount you can contribute (or elect to defer from taxes for a year) is $7,000; however, beginning in 1988 this maximum will be adjusted for increases in the Consumer Price Index.

DISADVANTAGES OF TAX-DEFERRAL SHELTERS

Although it is highly recommended that all average wage earners consider tax-deferral shelter plans—namely IRAs and 401 (K)s—as a strategy for supplementing their regular retirement income, it should be understood that this particular strategy may not be 'ideal' for everyone in every type of circumstance. In the first place, these two plans reduce a household's current cash flow. Circumstances at a particular time may require all of the cash that a household can generate. Whenever this is the case, a contribution to an IRA or a 401 (K) plan could adversely affect members of the household for years in the future. In the second place, as a result of the decrease in the number of tax brackets under the Tax Reform Act of 1986, more workers may remain in the same tax bracket after their retirement. For these workers, taxable investments such as stocks, CDs, or municipal bonds outside a tax-deferral plan may be a better proposition. For example, if you are currently between the ages of forty-five and fifty-five and you expect your tax bracket to decline from 28 percent now to 15 percent after retirement, then a tax-deferral plan should be in your best interest. If, however, you expect to remain in the 28 percent tax bracket after your retirement, current investment in long-term municipal bonds would be better.

KEY DECISIONS

For persons in retirement, not only income is important. The stability and indefinite duration of this income are important as well, because no one knows how long the retirement will last. This means that some decisions on retirement income should be made early in one's career, while others can be made during retirement itself. A decision on investment in securities is a good example. The results of all these decisions will have a significant impact on the retiree's income, and even though the emphasis will be placed on high income and safety of principal in these results, the retiree should always consider the factor of risk and the indefinite duration of retirement.

In addition to earnings from investments in securities and tax shelters, there are indeed other sources for supplementing retirement income. For example, an individual can invest in real estate, various commercial ventures, or the financing of the mortgage on a previously owned house. The important thing for you as a prospective retiree is to analyze your needs and circumstances— both now and in the future—to the best of your ability, and to relate all of these to your financial options for retirement.

Fortunately, recent legislation provides you and other potential retirees with more time to make key decisions on financing retirement, and the opportunity to generate more funds to use in that financing. These advantages stem from the enactment of federal legislation which bars virtually all employers from enforcing a mandatory retirement age, and similar laws in thirteen states, including such populous states as California, Florida, New Jersey, and New York. The major exceptions to the federal law, which became effective January 1, 1987, are state and local government exemptions for firefighters and law enforcement officers, and college and university personnel. The federal law also allows companies to enforce mandatory retirement at age sixty-five on high-level executives whose private pensions exceed $44,000 per year.

13·

Credit: Planning And Understanding Its Use

For the purpose of this discussion, look upon credit as simply the promise to pay in the future for purchases of goods and services in the present, and to pay back funds received as loans. In a previous chapter, we discussed the form of credit that involved paying back funds received as loans. We explained, for example, how an individual could borrow funds for the purpose of investing those funds with a view toward achieving a financial return sufficient to enable the individual to pay back the borrowed funds and realize a net gain. In this chapter, we shall stress the planning and understanding of that aspect of credit in which individuals promise to pay in the future in order to buy goods and services that they are either unable to pay for at the present, or do not wish to pay for at the present.

While most of us, at some time during our adult lives, find ourselves using credit, we still look upon credit as "going into debt," and for the most part, we dislike the idea of being in debt. Perhaps this idea is more emotional than logical. Experience shows that the use of credit, or "going into debt," can result in a higher standard of living for the household. Thus training in personal money management actually suggests that *there are times when the household should use credit*. In a sense, therefore, credit is a tool of personal money management, and, like all other tools, it should be used only after a certain amount of planning and analysis have taken place. Moreover, it should be related to the use of other tools, and it should be controlled. Specifically, you should always determine the household's need for credit; research the kinds of credit that are available; understand the ways of computing the cost of credit; be knowledgeable about the credit process; and be aware of the potential problems that can result from the use of credit.

Aside from providing you with an immediate economic gain, credit adds flexibility to personal money management because it enables you to obtain goods and services when they are needed most, and makes it easier to pay for these items within your overall financial plan. For the average family, credit is needed most when the financial demands of the family are at their peak and the income of the family is still relatively low. Later, when the family's income is higher, payments for credit received earlier can be made more conveniently.

DECIDING TO BUY ON CREDIT

Today, the inclination to use **credit** is based upon our growing demand for **durable goods** as our income rises. Our demand for a larger number and wider range of durable goods increases as our leisure time increases and our tastes change. We desire new and improved products as technology provides them, and we prefer present consumption over future consumption. Of course, a partner in our inclination to use credit is the willingness of **vendors** and financial institutions to finance our increasing demand for these new products and services.

- **credit:** the promise to pay in the future in order to buy in the present.
- **durable goods:** manufactured products capable of long use, such as refrigerators, automobiles, and various household appliances.
- **vendors:** companies that sell.

Advantages

While there is little doubt about the advantages of using credit, many people are still uncertain about when they should use it. Most of us want more goods and services than we have money to pay for; some of us, though, fear committing a part of our future income because we're afraid that our expected income might fall short of meeting all of our financial needs.

IMPACT OF TAX REFORM ACT OF 1986

We used to have two partners in buying in credit. One was the ever-accommodating seller of goods, services, and loanable funds. The other was Uncle Sam, who formerly shared the cost of our credit by permitting us to deduct a portion of the interest charges when filing our federal income taxes. With the passage of the Tax Reform Act of 1986, Uncle Sam's participation as a partner began to diminish in 1987, and will disappear completely in 1991. Specifically, the deductible portion of consumer credit cost drops to 40 percent in 1988, then to 20 percent in 1989, to 10 percent in 1990, and to zero percent in 1991.

There is one major exception to the end of this partnership with Uncle Sam. The cost of borrowing in which the loan is secured by a mortgage on a first or second home is still tax-deductible. Even in this instance, however, you should be familiar with the rules on which types of home-secured borrowing costs are fully deductible. For example, interest on any loan secured by a first or second residence is fully deductible if the total amount of debt secured by the house does not exceed the original purchase price of the house plus the cost of improvements. Beyond this, the amount would be deductible only if the proceeds of the loan were to be used for medical or educational purposes. These loans will be discussed in detail later in this chapter.

Even though you may be able to buy everything you need with cash, there are still several reasons why it may be to your advantage to buy some of these things on credit. One reason is to establish a good credit record. The time will come when you and your family will need to purchase an item on credit, such as a home or a car. You might also need to borrow money one day to finance your childrens' college education. When such a time does arrive, your success in getting the item may well depend on whether you have a good credit record. Another reason to buy on credit is to make money, surprising as that seems. This would be the case if you have a current investment opportunity that requires cash, and the financial return on this investment exceeds the finance charge on a credit purchase that you could have paid for with the same cash.

INSTALLMENT CREDIT

Installment credit is a loan with a fixed limit within which the consumer must make a series of equal payments. Most such loans are made for a period of one to three years and are paid monthly. In most sales on the installment plan, **title** to the item purchased does not pass to the buyer until the final payment is made. Failure to make the payments gives the vendor the right to take back the item. Most people use installment credit to buy such items as automobiles, home furnishings, large appliances, and, in recent years, such services as travel and education. When goods and services are purchased in this manner, the buyer is in fact borrowing money.

When you decide to buy something on installment, you should shop carefully among possible lenders for the best rates and terms that suit your plans for repayment.

A key item in the terms for repayment on installment loans is the **annual percentage rate** (APR), which is usually fairly reliable for comparing lenders' credit terms. When you decide to buy an item on installment, first find out the APR charged by the merchant and compare that to the rates charged by various financial institutions, including your credit union if you belong to one. All lenders are required by federal law (Truth in Lending Act of 1968) to state the cost of their credit in terms of the finance charge and the APR, thus making it easier for customers to compare the credit terms of various lenders.

- **title:** evidence that a person is the legal owner of property.
- **annual percentage rate:** the cost of credit on a yearly basis expressed as a percentage.

Another key factor in installment buying is the finance charge, which is the total dollar amount paid for the privilege of buying on credit. This dollar amount is ascertained by adding your down payment, which usually must be made in cash, to all the periodic payments scheduled by the loan agreement and comparing this total with the cash price of the merchandise. The difference between your total outlay and the price of the merchandise is actually the cost of buying the item on installment or of borrowing the money. The lower the amount you pay weekly or monthly, the higher the cost of buying on installment or borrowing money. This is because the interest rate is applied to a higher unpaid balance.

In summary, whenever you decide to buy a costly item, consider the following guidelines:

1. Comparison shop to get the lowest cash price possible.
2. If buying on credit, find out the APR charged by the vendor, along with other items in the repayment plan.
3. Comparison shop again—this time among lenders or the various financial institutions. Be sure to focus on the APR.
4. Compare the terms—especially the APR—of the vendor and those of various lending institutions.
5. Find the true price of buying the item on installment or borrowing the money to make the purchase, and decide whether it is in your best interest to buy it on credit.
6. If the final decision is to buy the item on installment, select the terms that best fit your plans for repayment.

CHARGE ACCOUNTS: REVOLVING CREDIT

Many stores now offer the consumer a charge account, which resembles the line of credit that many commercial banks offer to business firms. This type of account is called a revolving charge account. With a typical revolving account, you may pay either the full amount due in thirty days with no service charge (or interest), or you may elect to pay a stipulated amount each month with an interest charge on the unpaid balance. You may charge additional items to your account as long as you remain within the maximum amount set by the store's credit office. Each month, you receive a statement that shows the unpaid balance, the service charge computed on the balance at the beginning of each monthly billing period, and the amount of the monthly installment due. As the balance decreases, the monthly installment due is lowered.

Different stores use different methods for computing the unpaid or outstanding balance on the revolving charge account. The three widely used methods are based on the previous balance, the unpaid balance, and the average daily balance. Under the previous balance method, the creditor gives you no credit for payments made during the billing period. For example, assume that you owe $200 on your charge account, and that your payment in a particular month is $50. The previous balance method would still require you to pay a finance charge (interest) on the entire $200. Using an interest rate of 1.5 percent a month, the finance charge would be $3.00. With the average daily balance method, the creditor would add your balance for each day in the billing period and then divide by the number of days in the billing period. Thus, if the creditor uses the average daily balance method, and if you make your $50 payment by the middle of the month, your average daily balance would probably amount to $175 and your finance charge would be about $2.63. With the unpaid balance method, the creditor adds finance charges after subtracting payments during the billing period. Using the same example as above, you would get credit for your $50 payment, and would be charged interest only on the remaining $150, for a finance charge of $2.25. As you can see, the unpaid balance method is the most favorable to the consumer. Regardless of the method used, the Truth in Lending Law requires the creditor to indicate on his bills the method used in computing the customer's balance and to state the rate of interest in terms of an annual percentage rate.

CREDIT CARDS

Among other devices designed to simplify the extension of credit is the credit card. Millions of Americans carry embossed plastic cards issued by commercial banks, oil companies, retail stores, chains, and firms offering entertainment. Credit cards can be used to buy clothing, hardware, appliances, furniture, recreational equipment, and gasoline. They can also be used to pay for restaurant meals, car rentals, airline tickets, motel rooms, and medical services—even to make charitable contributions and to obtain cash. The widespread and growing acceptance of credit cards by vendors and consumers now makes it possible for people to acquire most of the necessities and comforts of life—and to travel all over the world—without carrying much cash or writing checks. When used prudently, credit cards are very convenient.

The Billing and Cost of Using a Card

Credit card charges are billed monthly. The bill shows the amount due, the date on which the amount is due, the date of each charge, the seller submitting the charge, and other pertinent information. However, because of the multitude of different credit cards offered today, the various credit terms, and the different ways of interpreting these terms, it is difficult to compute the true cost of using any credit card. The following costs pertain to the most widely used cards today, although even these costs are subject to frequent changes.

Annual Fee. This is a flat fee charged once a year for the use of the card. Currently, this fee ranges upward from $15. A few card issuers charge no fee.

Grace Period. There is usually about a month between the day you charge a purchase and the day that interest charges begin. Some cards have no grace period.

Interest Rate. The average interest rate is about 17.9 percent, although the range is fairly wide. A few lenders charge floating rates, which vary with market interest rates.

Information on these factors is essential to making decisions on the use of a credit card and the selection of a credit card. Often, however, this information is missing or obscured in the card offerings. Despite these problems, there are certain factors about the use of a card that you can control. For example, if you pay the total amount due on each billing, you don't have to concern yourself with the confusion on the interest rate. On the other hand, if it is more advantageous for you to make only a minimum payment on the total amount due, then you do need to concern yourself with the interest rate.

Affinity Cards

One of the recent developments in the issuance of credit cards is an arrangement in which a nonbanking group asks a bank to issue a special type of credit card to the group's members. This special type of card is commonly referred to as an "affinity card." These groups now consist of alumni organizations, churches, labor unions, and special citizen organizations. The group usually gets a portion of the annual fee, and sometimes a percentage of the charge balance. While this arrangement can assist the group in its fund-raising efforts, the individual group member usually pays more than he or she would for a card directly issued by a bank. The exception to this experience may be the affinity cards issued by labor unions.

Bank Cards

Among the most popular credit cards are those issued by commercial banks. Banks offer these cards to customers with good credit records. Most banks that issue credit cards are associated with one or both of the two major bank credit card systems, Visa and Master Card. The cards issued by these systems are honored in stores throughout the United States and in many of the hotels abroad. Currently, Visa and Master Card account for nearly 95 percent of the total credit card business. About 200 small independent banks also operate credit card plans. Because bank credit card slips are the equivalent of cash, many participating merchants find them preferable to the consumer's checks or to revolving charge accounts. The expense of credit investigations, bookkeeping, and collections are assumed by card-issuing banks.

Advantages

The use of credit cards has a number of advantages. Travelers find that a card eliminates the risk of carrying large sums of cash to pay for food, lodging, and other goods and services. Many motels and restaurants do not accept personal checks. In paying for an item with a credit card, the consumer gets a copy of the slip showing the credit card payment. This document can be retained as a proof-of-purchase for items such as gasoline, and other transactions for which receipts are not usually issued. Many people find that credit receipts can be useful when defending certain deductions during a tax audit.

HOME EQUITY LOANS

"How would you like to have thousands of dollars of available credit at your fingertips to use when and how you like? All you have to do is be a homeowner!"

"Put the equity in your home to work for you. Apply now to get a line of credit that you can use for anything you want— new furniture, tuition, travel, emergencies—anytime you want."

Advertisements like these are commonplace as more lenders offer **home equity** loans or "home equity lines of credit." These credit lines are extremely popular. Creditors like them because the credit they're extending is secured by a valuable asset—a consumer's home. Consumers like them because, by using the equity in their homes, they often qualify at comparatively low interest rates for a sizable amount of credit. And this credit is conveniently available to consumers to use when and how they please.

Home equity loans are becoming very popular in light of the Tax Reform Act of 1986. Under this tax law, the deductibility of interest paid on unsecured extensions of credit will be phased out. Consumers may be able to deduct interest, however, on debts secured by their homes. But whether interest may be deducted—and the extent to which it may be deducted—depends on circumstances specific to each consumer (for example, when the debt was incurred, and—if the debt exceeds the purchase price and cost of improvements to the home—how the credit is used). Therefore, consumers should consult a tax expert to determine what interest, if any, is deductible.

What Is a Home Equity Loan

A home equity loan is a type of mortgage loan. You must use your home as security for the credit line, so if you default on your payments you run a serious risk of losing your home. Because their homes are used as collateral, many consumers use their credit lines

---

• **home equity:** the difference between the fair market value of your home and your outstanding mortgage balance.

only for major purchases or expenditures, such as education or home improvements, and not for small day-to-day expenses.

With a home equity loan you can borrow when you want to—although some plans may require you to take an advance when you open the account. Like a credit card account, you are approved for a maximum amount of credit (your "credit limit") that you can use from time to time to make purchases and obtain cash. Your credit limit on your home equity loan will be determined in part by the amount of equity you have in your home. By giving the creditor a security interest in your home, you tie up that equity, which may prevent you from using your home as collateral for other borrowing. Moreover, if you sell your home you will be required to pay off your home equity loan at that time.

The application process for a home equity loan is usually extensive, very similar to the process when you buy a home. It also can be expensive, involving the payment of substantial fees not normally required for unsecured credit.

What Costs Are Involved in Obtaining a Home Equity Loan?

You may have to pay a number of fees to obtain a home equity credit line. These fees are charged to establish the line of credit, regardless of how much credit you use or whether you use the plan at all. For example:

1. You may have to pay an application fee. You may also have to pay additional fees to cover such items as a credit report and an appraisal, although sometimes these fees are included in the application fee. These fees are usually not refundable if you are turned down for credit.

2. Home equity loans may involve up-front charges, such as **points** (one point equals one percent of your credit limit) or an origination fee (a charge that is often figured by multiplying your

---

• **points:** additional fees that may be charged in home equity loans and are often collected at closing; a point equals one percent of the amount financed.

credit limit by a specified amount—for example, one or two percent).

3. Home equity loans also involve **closing costs**—fees for preparing and filing the mortgage, as well as for a title search, taxes, insurance, and attorneys' fees.

4. Many plans also charge an annual membership or participation fee.

These costs add up, and before you know it you could end up paying several hundred dollars—and in some cases significantly more—in up-front, one-time costs. If you only borrow a small amount on your credit line, the up-front charges and closing costs you pay can substantially increase the cost of your loan.

Shopping for a Home Equity Loan

In shopping for a home equity loan, you'll want to compare the costs involved in establishing the credit line. You'll also want to keep the following in mind:

1. The rates for home equity loans are generally lower than the rates charged for other types of credit. Because you're giving the lender a security interest in your home, the lender's risk is lower; therefore, lower rates can be offered. Such interest savings—which you may not get with other forms of credit—could prove to balance off the initial costs involved in establishing home equity lines.

2. Sometimes creditors advertise rates for home equity loans that are unusually low. Often these are temporary, introductory rates that will increase after a specified time. Therefore, it is important to find out how long the introductory rate will be in effect and what the rate will be after the introductory rate ends.

3. Most home equity loans involve variable interest rates rather

---

• **closing costs:** fees payable immediately before you receive title to your home. These fees include costs associated with the attorney, preparing and filing the mortgage, taxes, title search, credit report, survey, insurance, etc.

than fixed rates. A **variable rate** is tied to an index such as a prime rate or a Treasury bill rate, and changes as the index changes. Furthermore, lenders add a **margin**, such as 2 percent, to the index rate to determine the rate you will pay. Since the interest rate charged in a variable rate plan may change, you'll want to find out what index the lender uses, the margin the lender adds to the index rate, and how much and how often the rate can change. Fortunately, a provision in the Competitive Equality Banking Act of 1987 requires interest-rate limits on all adjustable (variable) rate mortgages and home equity loans.

4. Under variable rate plans you also will want to know what happens when the rate changes. For example, if the rate rises, will your payment amount increase? Will the lender be permitted under the terms of your agreement to apply the higher rate to the balance you have outstanding at the time of the rate increase?

5. Check to see when and under what circumstances the lender can change the terms and conditions of your credit line.

6. Home equity loans do not usually involve a "free period" (also called a grace period). Thus, you will be charged interest right away—usually from the day you draw on the line, or the day the transaction is posted to your account.

7. Find out if the plan involves transaction fees (a fee charged every time you draw on your line). These fees will not be reflected in an advertised annual percentage rate.

You'll want to consider all this information when deciding whether to apply for a home equity loan. Ask the creditor for this information, and for the answers to any other questions you might have.

- **variable rate:** an interest rate that changes periodically in relation to an index; payments may increase or decrease accordingly.
- **margin:** the number of percentage points the lender adds to the index rate to determine the interest rate to be charged.

How Do Home Equity Loans Work?

How is your credit limit determined?   Your credit limit on your home equity loan depends in part on the amount of equity in your home. Equity is the fair market value of your home (usually determined by an appraisal) less your outstanding mortgage balance. For example, if the fair market value of your home is $100,000 and your mortgage balance is $40,000, the amount of equity in your home is $60,000. Many lenders offer credit limits of approximately 75 percent of the appraised value of your home, less any existing mortgage. So, in this example, you may be eligible for a $35,000 credit line. (You arrive at this figure by taking 75 percent of $100,000, the fair market value of your home. This gives you $75,000. You then subtract $40,000, the amount of your outstanding mortgage balance, from $75,000 to arrive at the $35,000 figure). In determining your credit limit, however, a lender also will consider your ability to repay, looking at such factors as your income, debts, and other obligations.

How is the credit line accessed?   Most home equity lines are accessed by using a special package of checks. Some lines can also be accessed by a credit card. Many plans require that advances on your credit line be no less than a minimum amount, for example $500. If you draw on your line for less than the minimum amount, the lender may refuse to pay your check, or you may be required to pay a fee.

What types of payment arrangements are involved?   Payment arrangements for home equity loans differ from creditor to creditor. Some plans require minimum payments that include a portion of the principal (the amount you borrowed) and interest. Others require payments of "interest only" until the plan ends.

"Interest only" payments may give you a false impression of your true ability to repay the loan once the credit plan ends and principal and interest payments become due—especially if interest rates have risen during the life of the loan. For example, interest only payments on a $20,000 account balance at an interest rate of 10 percent would be approximately $167 per month. If rates rise to 15 percent during the life of the plan, then your interest payments would increase to $250 per month.

No matter what your payment arrangements are during the life of the loan, when the loan ends you may be required to pay off the entire balance owed at that time. This final payment is known as a "balloon payment." In the interest only payment example, you would not have paid off any principal during the life of the loan; consequently, when the loan ends you would have the entire $20,000 balance remaining. Had you made principal and interest payments over the life of the loan—rather than interest only payments—you would have paid down a portion of the original $20,000 principal amount, resulting in a smaller balance outstanding when the loan ends.

You must be prepared to pay off the outstanding balance when the loan ends—for example, by refinancing with the lender or obtaining financing from another lender. In the example used above, refinancing the outstanding balance of $20,000 at an interest rate of 15 percent—assuming a ten-year amortization—would result in monthly payments of approximately $323.

Understanding your repayment obligations is critical. Therefore, you'll want to seriously consider your ability to repay before entering into a home equity loan.

Your Right to Cancel Your Home Equity Loan

When you open a home equity loan, you enter into a transaction that puts your home at risk. Because this is an important decision, federal law gives you three days—usually from when the account is opened—to cancel the credit line. If, for any reason, you change your mind within this time, the creditor must cancel the security interest in your home and return all fees paid in opening the account.

Alternatives to Home Equity Loans

If you need to borrow money, but aren't sure whether a home equity loan is right for you, there are alternatives. For example:

1. You might want to explore the more traditional type of mortgage loan, where a fixed amount of credit is extended in one lump sum (rather than on an as-needed basis), with a set payment schedule. These mortgages may have higher interest rates, but these rates are usually fixed. This avoids the possibility that your payments will increase should interest rates rise.

2. You may want to consider borrowing money from unsecured credit lines. These are often available with your credit cards (cash advances) or as part of your checking account (**overdraft checking** privileges). While interest rates on such lines are usually higher than on home equity loans, you will not be required to give your home as security.

Remember . . .

If you're in the market for a home equity loan, you'll want to shop carefully, making sure that you understand the costs involved in obtaining and using a home equity loan, as well as the terms for repayment. Most importantly, since a home equity line involves putting your home at risk, you'll want to carefully consider whether such a credit plan suits your needs.

Remember, all taxpayers who receive home equity loans must complete IRS Form 8598 when filing their federal income tax.

COST OF CREDIT

Credit costs can be very confusing, partly because of the many different terms used to express these costs. Among the familiar terms are interest rate, discount rate, service charge or fee, finance charge, and—in the case of some direct loans—a charge of so many dollars per $100 of the loan. It is also possible for two loans with the same APR to have different finance charges because of differences in the other terms of the loan.

True Interest Rate

A very simple method of comparing credit cost is to compute the cost on the basis of true interest rate, that is, on the basis of the amount of money you actually have use of during the period of the loan. (For further information, see the publication *What Truth in*

---

* **overdraft checking:** a checking account associated with a line of credit that allows a person to write checks for more than the actual balance in the account, with a finance charge on the overdraft.

Lending Means to You, Board of Governors of the Federal Reserve System, Washington, D.C., June 1981.) To illustrate, assume that you can borrow $100 on terms requiring you to repay the $100 plus $6 in finance charges in a single payment one year later. The $6 finance charge is equal to 6 percent of $100, thus you are paying a true annual rate of 6 percent. Now, in a different situation, let us assume that you borrow the same $100, but this time the bank **discounts your note** for $100. This means that you receive $94 to use instead of $100. The finance charge on this loan is still $6. However, you have $6 less to use during the year. The true interest rate, in this case on $94, is approximately 6.5 percent.

Most personal loans obtained by consumers, however, are installment loans rather than single-payment loans. When one borrows $100 for a year, with a finance charge of $6, he is expected to repay the loan in equal monthly installments. Since the borrower is required to begin repaying the loan within a month and to continue to repay the loan throughout the year, he has, on the average, actually had the use of only about one-half of the money originally borrowed. In this case, the true annual interest rate is actually almost twice as large as that on the single-payment loan, or about 12 percent.

Any table that purports to show how much credit can cost is only a guide. Rates vary considerably and lenders have different ways of computing and assessing interest charges—although the APR is designed to make comparison easier for the borrower.

Credit Insurance

In negotiating credit with the borrower, the lender is likely to suggest that the borrower purchase credit life or credit accident and health insurance through the lender's own firm. Such insurance assures repayment of the loan or any portion outstanding if the borrower dies or becomes disabled.

• **discount a note:** the lender deducts the interest amount from the face value of the note and remits the remainder to the borrower.

When applying for credit, the creditor may try to pressure you into buying credit insurance as a condition for granting the credit. While in certain states it is legal for a creditor to require borrowers to obtain credit insurance, federal laws prohibit lenders from specifying that it be purchased from a specific source. Moreover, when credit insurance is required, the Truth in Lending Act mandates that its cost be included in the annual percentage rate quoted for the loan.

You should determine for yourself whether you should buy credit insurance. If you have sufficient regular life insurance or assets with which to repay existing loans in the event of your death or disability, then credit insurance may be a poor purchase.

On certain loans, particularly for mobile homes and mortgages, the lender may require that you obtain credit insurance. In such cases, however, the lender must give you the option of furnishing the required coverage through your existing policies or purchasing the required coverage from an insurer authorized to do business in that state.

YOUR CREDIT RECORD

It is important to establish a credit record as a vital component of personal money management. A good credit record allows you to buy things on credit, and thus essentially have more money available to you.

Establishing the Record

In general, people establish good credit records by paying all of their bills and paying these bills on time. Failure to do so results in a poor credit record and eventually closes the door to any future credit, including loans from agencies of the federal government or loans guaranteed by these agencies. The practice of personal money management includes buying something on credit at an early stage in your economic career in order to establish a credit history; however, you should do so only if you have the capacity and discipline to repay the obligation and make the payments when they are due.

Unfortunately, there are times when an individual fails to meet his or her credit obligations despite having had the capacity to pay at the time the obligation was created. For example, people often have emergencies that force them to skip payments on bills in order to meet expenditures connected with the unexpected problems. It is also quite possible to forget to make a payment on a credit obligation. These and other unanticipated incidents might happen to anyone who has the good intention of paying his or her credit obligations. In the meantime, however, the missed payments are recorded by the creditor and sent to a credit bureau as part of your credit record, and subsequently become part of your credit report, which is requested by any seller considering your application for credit.

When payments on credit obligations are missed, most people offer an explanation to the creditor. Some of these creditors will record the explanation. Some will not. This difference in attitude or policy by the creditor can result in a good credit record or a not-so-good (or poor) credit record for the customer at the local credit bureau. Unfortunately, you, the credit customer, do not know which of these two actions has been taken until you decide to apply for credit again, and the report detailing your credit record is requested from the local credit bureau.

Federal Law on Credit Reports

If you apply for credit and your application is rejected, federal law now requires credit grantors to give you the reasons for the rejection. If you are told that a credit report is the major reason for the rejection, the credit grantor must give you the name of the credit bureau that provided the credit report. You can then arrange a meeting with that credit bureau to review the contents of your credit record or write the credit bureau to receive a copy of your credit report. The Fair Credit Reporting Act entitles you to the following:

1. to know the nature, substance, and sources of all data in your file;

2. to be accompanied by another person when you visit the credit bureau office;

3. to obtain all data from the credit reporting bureau without charge when you have been denied credit within the past thirty days;

4. to know who has received your file for credit purposes in the past six months, and for employment purposes in the past two years;
5. to have any information you consider incomplete or inaccurate rechecked;
6. to have information that cannot be substantiated, or is incorrect, removed;
7. to have those who received inaccurate or incomplete or disputed information notified of changes;
8. to have a statement placed in your file telling your side of the story if rechecking doesn't settle a dispute;
9. to have no adverse information in your file older than seven years, or in case of bankruptcy, fourteen years.

Revised Credit Reports

If the unfavorable information in your file at the credit bureau is accurate, you may have to soften the impact of your credit reports by submitting a short statement to the bureau citing the reasons why you have a poor credit record. For example, missed payments resulting from extended periods of unemployment or illness may persuade the credit grantor to be more lenient when viewing your credit report than it would without this explanation. If the bureau accepts your explanation for the missed payments, the bureau might send a revised credit report on your record to credit grantors who received the unfavorable report in the past.

Other Reasons for Credit Denial

In addition to denying credit on the basis of an unfavorable credit report, a credit grantor may choose to deny you credit for any one of the following reasons:

1. inability to verify employment;
2. length of stay at current residence;
3. behavior of balance in bank account;
4. insufficient income;
5. excessive financial obligations;
6. insufficient credit history.

Although the aforementioned factors may be used to deny credit initially, most of them can be countered successfully within a reasonable period of time if you stay at one job for a while and conduct your financial affairs in a fairly orderly manner. Even the problem of insufficient income can be overcome by reducing your budget and credit needs to fit your current earnings. All creditors do not use the same criteria or guidelines for denying credit. However, you can avoid many of the problems associated with the denial of credit by adhering to the principles of personal money management and by using the privilege of credit as a means of extending this management.

PROBLEMS WITH CREDIT

Clearly, the amount of credit that an individual can carry without risking future embarrassment, loss of purchase, or even **bankrupt-cy**, may be less than some household borrowers realize. On the other hand, the ease of obtaining credit can understandably lead to repayment commitments hazardously large in relation to income. This often reduces the borrower's capacity to meet emergencies that might take place in the near future. There might be numerous instances in which the expectations of both the borrower and the lender tend to be overly optimistic.

One of the dangers associated with the use of credit is the temptation of **impulse buying**. There is often a great temptation to buy things you can't really afford at the moment, with the expectation that you will have the money when the payment is due. The risks in such instances are that other pressing expenses may arise and that the items purchased on credit may be repossessed because of your inability to keep up payments.

Another source of trouble is the extra cost of using credit. Buying on credit usually involves payment of interest, and this extra cost can quickly accumulate into a sizable sum.

- **bankruptcy:** an individual's status in which a state law usually allows the individual's creditors to claim his or her assets for repayment of debts (with certain assets or a portion thereof expected).
- **impulse buying:** unplanned spending or buying on a whim.

How much debt can you afford to have? Unfortunately, there is no safety rule that fits all individuals and families in all situations. Some analysts suggest an individual have a ratio of debt to such factors as take-home pay and total income. The real answer, however, lies in your particular financial situation and involves consideration of the following factors.

1. How much is your take-home pay and other income?
2. How much do you normally spend?
3. How much do you owe already?
4. What are your future needs and obligations?
5. What resources do you have?
6. How secure is your income?

When a household is reported by a creditor to a credit bureau as a chronic **delinquent** in making repayments, or is forced to suffer the embarrassment of having a credit purchase repossessed, it means that the household has ignored a number of warning signals indicating the use of too much credit. Such signals usually consist of one or more of the following:

1. The household begins to use funds set aside for insurance premiums to pay for such essentials as utilities.
2. The household begins to pay only the minimum due each month on various charge accounts.
3. Creditors begin to send reminders about overdue payments to the household.
4. The household begins to take out new personal loans to pay old personal loans and to make payments that are past due on various charge accounts.
5. The household begins to consistently skip putting aside the amount budgeted for savings.

Most of us use credit at one time or another in our lives, and since credit is one of the most valuable assets we can have, it makes good sense for us to protect our households, our jobs, and our futures by

---

• **delinquent:** a debtor who is behind in making payments on a debt and has made no satisfactory arrangement with the lender.

using it wisely. Some analysts suggest that our credit payment should not exceed 20 percent of our take-home pay after rent or mortgage payments. This rule-of-thumb limitation is doubtless related to many averages in the typical family budget, and could vary from household to household depending upon the household's discipline. However, it might also help if we keep in mind that our objective should be to borrow the least we need, not the most we can get.

If you have not been able to observe the rules on limitation of credit, or if you are victimized by an unfortunate incident that threatens your ability to repay loans, you should contact the lender immediately to discuss the situation and possibly arrange for a reduced payment or a renegotiated loan. It cannot be emphasized too strongly that you should communicate with the lender as soon as possible.

Depending upon the circumstances, you may be charged additional fees called late charges, the lender may **garnishee** your wages (in some states), the item purchased may be repossessed, and the lender may, on a mortgage, **foreclose** on your home. Your loan or credit contract will specify the rights of the lender to recover the borrowed funds if you are late with your repayments. If you do not understand how these remedies work, you should ask questions before you sign the contract.

Regaining A Good Credit Rating

A consumer who has a poor credit rating may regain a good credit rating by paying off all delinquent bills and settling all credit disputes. Each time a delinquent bill is satisfied, the consumer should request a letter from the creditor stating that the bill has been paid. The consumer should request the creditor to send a copy of the letter to the local credit bureau. To make sure that a copy of the letter is sent, the consumer should send a copy of his or her own

---

- **garnishee:** a legal action taken by a creditor to secure payment of a debt by attaching the debtor's salary or other income.
- **foreclose:** a creditor sells property in the possession of the debtor to use the proceeds to liquidate or reduce the debt.

letter. If, for some reason, the creditor fails to write such a letter, or is late in doing so, the consumer should send a copy of the receipt for payment of the bill to the creditor.

In addition to taking the aforementioned steps to regain your good rating, or at least improve your rating, you should do the following:

1. Use and maintain in good standing a checking or savings account.

2. Apply for a department store or gasoline credit card and pay each billing on time.

3. Join a credit union, take a loan, and repay the funds promptly.

PERSONAL BANKRUPTCY: A LAST RESORT

Bankruptcy may be viewed as the financial condition of a person or corporation that indicates inability to pay debts, often because of an over-extension of credit. Relief from bankruptcy is provided by the Federal Bankruptcy Act, although every state has its own **statutes** on the matter. Two sections of the federal law, which constitute what are commonly referred to as the wage earner plan and straight bankruptcy, are particularly relevant to consumers who are unable to cope with their debts.

The Wage Earner Plan

If you are a wage earner (an individual whose principal income is derived from wages, salaries, and commissions) you can voluntarily file a **petition** that declares that you are insolvent or unable to pay your debts as they mature and that you would like to present a plan to scale down or extend the **maturity** of your debts. Bankruptcy is not the same as insolvency. Insolvency, as defined by federal code, means that the total present value of all the debtor's property is

---

* **statutes:** laws established by the act of a legislature.
* **petition:** a written request to a court or to a judge for the granting of some remedy or relief.
* **maturity:** the date when the debt is due.

insufficient to pay his or her debts. Thus, a debtor may be insolvent without being bankrupt. The advantage of this plan is that you can avoid the procedure and stigma of straight bankruptcy. Since your only asset as a wage earner is your future earning power, this plan allows you to turn over that asset to your creditors.

When you, the debtor, present your plan to the court, a meeting is held to gain approval. If your creditors accept the plan and the court is convinced of its fairness and feasibility, it becomes binding, and your future earnings are controlled by the court to carry out the plan. From that point, you must systematically meet a revised set of obligations to reduce your original debt.

In proceedings with a bankruptcy court, you must have a lawyer, so there is little point in filing a wage earner plan if your debts are much less than $1,000. Otherwise, lawyer fees and court costs would make it too costly. Under a wage earner plan, however, lawyer fees (ranging from less than $100 to $400) are controlled by the court and can be paid off in monthly installments over the extended debt payment period. Bankruptcy courts are federal institutions and can be found through your nearest U.S. District Court. Some local bar associations have pamphlets on wage earner plans.

Straight Bankruptcy

Straight bankruptcy is a legal process whereby one's assets, except for certain personal items, are collected by the court and sold for cash, and the proceeds distributed among the creditors. You, the debtor, are then discharged from your unsatisfied debts. No discharge will be granted to a petitioner for bankruptcy who has received a previous discharge from debts within a six-year period.

Even though you may not see any possible way of ever paying off huge debts, filing for bankruptcy ought to be among your last alternatives. For one thing, bankruptcy does not result in the discharge of all your provable debts. You cannot be released, for example, from any federal tax claims or taxes levied by any state, county, district, or municipality. You will also lose whatever assets you have that are not exempt under state laws. Finally, there is still a stigma attached to straight bankruptcy. The bankrupt person is often stamped as a bad credit risk by some credit-granting institutions, and people in small towns are still distrustful of people who go bankrupt.

People with certain types of income should consider matters very carefully before filing for bankruptcy because they may be "judgment-proof" even though they are hopelessly in debt. Some people in judgment-proof categories are those receiving any kind of special government assistance such as Social Security (retirement, disability, or widow's benefits), workers' compensation (benefits received for a disabling on-the-job accident or illness), or unemployment compensation. Income from these sources cannot be garnisheed or taken away from the recipient to satisfy a debt.

FINAL CONSIDERATIONS

Decisions to use credit reflect a number of factors, such as your household's needs, goals, income, and values. Sensibly used, credit can be an important tool of money management, and effectively used, it can help your household to enjoy a higher standard of living. On the other hand, credit can become addictive and can result in loss of reputation, loss of collateral, court action, garnishment of salary, and even bankruptcy.

Before using credit, you should evaluate very carefully your household's financial condition and other options for satisfying the household's needs and wants. Credit is not more money. It's just a convenience that lets your household enjoy now certain benefits that must be paid for later on.

Finally, you should understand that credit is usually not free. It is paid for by interest charges that vary with the type of lender, kind of credit, and time period involved. Interest charges are no longer deductible as they were before the Tax Reform Act of 1986, and while lenders are vigorously seeking credit customers, they are also vigorously pressing for payments due.

Try not to postpone any payments due on a credit obligation, because such postponements are apt to continue and result in a problem. If you are unable to make a scheduled payment because of unforeseen difficulties, contact your creditor immediately and discuss your payment problems.

14 ·

Converting Principles To Practices In Personal Money Management

There is a great deal of literature on such topics as personal economics, managing your own money, personal finance, and personal money management, and much of it embodies a core of principles that is easy to understand and easy to follow. This book presesnts this core of principles throughout the discussions in the various chapters, and attempts to explain how such principles can be put into practice in your household. As yet there is no formal theory of personal money management; however, every effort has been made to present the information in this book in an orderly fashion, and at the same time, to offer enough depth on each subject to make you effective in managing your household's finances.

This chapter is specifically designed to assist you in converting the essentials in previous chapters into the practice of personal money management. In some respects, this objective might be viewed as a summary of the book itself. To be sure, the discussion that follows may contain some summarizing of previous information. Its real purpose, however, is to reemphasize the importance of the core of principles in money management, to tie these principles together as much as possible, and to present all of this in a manner that will make sense to you and give you the necessary confidence to manage your household's money.

YOUR STAKE IN PERSONAL MONEY MANAGEMENT

All of us want to live comfortably now and in the future. However, we are not likely to live as comfortably during the initial years of our adulthood as during the years that follow, because experience shows that our income during these early years is lower, and increases as we become older. Most of us are reasonably certain that part of this steady increase in income will come from periodic increments in our wages and salaries. Such increases, however, may not be sufficient to provide us with the standard and style of living we expect during various stages of our lives. Thus, as soon as we become responsible for our own financial support, we should begin to think about ways to increase our current income in order to live more comfortably in the early years of adulthood, and to satisfy those needs and wants in later years that may require more than the normal salary increases can provide.

In an effort to live more comfortably, many of us are inclined to buy more and more on credit. Sooner or later, however, our future buying is restricted because previous debts must be paid. In the final analysis, we recognize that our basic problem is the need for more income. This leaves us with two choices: to seek supplemental employment or to manage our current income in a manner that generates additional income.

After recognizing that your best bet for gaining additional income is to manage your current income, your next problem is to decide who is going to manage your money and when the management process should begin. If you are the average wage earner or a person with very modest financial resources, it is you who will manage your money because you cannot afford to hire a bank or a professional financial counselor. This means that you must train yourself to carry out all of the tasks that make up personal money management. You must find a way to monitor your expenditures and your cash flow. You must decide what your financial goals are and establish a timetable for achieving them. And you must read the financial sections of various newspapers and magazines in order to stay abreast of those developments that can affect your personal finances.

Additional Income for the Household

Many of us often ask ourselves, "Will I go through the rest of my life looking forward to receiving only one check on a periodic basis?" We also ask ourselves, "What happens when I get sick and cannot work for a few months? Does this mean that I won't have any income at all?" When we answer these questions for ourselves, we begin to realize how important it is to have additional sources of income. And when we understand that it is possible for us to create those sources through skilled management of our existing income, we ought to conclude that such management should begin now!

An Extra $60 Can Be Crucial

In certain conversations, you are likely to hear statements to the effect that money management is not worth the effort of the average wage earner, or that it is for people with big money—where the money management results in thousands of dollars of extra income. The implication is that the average wage earner has nothing to gain from the practice of personal money management. This philosophy is misguided; and to the extent that such a pilosophy is followed by average wage earners, people in this income group are not likely to raise their standards of living and may well be forced to forego opportunities that could be crucial to the futures of their families.

A review of the latter part of chapter 6 should not only dispel any doubts about the value of personal money management to the average wage earner, but also illustrate how crucial such an effort can be to the average wage earner's family. Extra earnings can be generated from savings—even the modest savings that are deposited in a passbook savings account—and can be important to you and to your family. A passbook savings account can produce additional income in amounts that are worthy of counting as a part of the household's regular income. The extra income from savings can be budgeted for goods and services that the family could not previously afford.

To further illustrate the critical effect that even a modest amount of additional income from personal money management can have on the future of a family, let's speculate on the possible use of $60 in interest income from $1,000 maintained in the family's passbook savings account during the past year. The family in question has three teenage children attending a high school in North Carolina that is scheduling a field trip to the National Institute of Health in Washington, D.C. The fare for each student is $60, and the family can spare only $120 from its budget for this purpose, which means that one of the family's children will be forced to miss the trip. In such a situation, is it not possible to think that personal money management might have produced a modest amount of additional income for a trip that could inspire a teenage member of the family to become a physician in the future?

As an average wage earner, your stake in personal money management is as big—perhaps even bigger—than that of people with higher salaries. This is simply because an additional $50 or $75 can mean more to your family's budget than an additional $1,000 means to a millionaire. As indicated previously, an additional $60 could affect the entire future of your household, whereas $5,000 would hardly be noticed by a millionaire. Because of this potential importance to you and your family, you should think seriously about learning personal money management and you should put this learning into practice now.

TOWARD ADDITIONAL INCOME

Although personal money management implies much more than gaining additional income, we cannot overlook the fact that the primary financial objective of the average wage earner *is* to gain additional income. Until very recently, a second or third job was the only means by which the average person could do so. The situation is significantly different now. Expanded financial markets, changes in regulations, great competition among financial institutions, and improved systems of communications, along with many other changes, now make it possible and convenient for the average wage earner to make money with his or her current income. Gaining additional income from current income is referred to as investing, and as a person interested in personal money management, you should make the subject of investing part of your core knowledge and one of your everyday concerns.

Money as a Competitor of Investments

If you are really serious about personal money management, then anytime that you have cash on you—in a straight checking account at the bank or stashed some place in your house—you are losing money. Of course, everybody needs to keep some cash available for those expenditures that require cash. Nevertheless, we should not forget that all money can be invested, and thus any money in excess of our petty cash needs is not producing additional income as it should.

One of the many theories in economics gives prominence to the so-called speculative motive for holding money. The idea is that individuals are likely to hold cash, thinking that interest rates will rise or that some other opportunity for financial gain will soon occur. Such a theory may or may not be true. However, even if yields on current investments are relatively low, you would still be foregoing additional income by holding the speculative resources in cash; and the longer you hold the cash waiting for a profitable opportunity, the more money you lose.

Because you do lose money when you hold it and because there are times when you need to hold money or accumulate money to be prepared to make a profitable investment, you are obviously faced with several problems. How long should you hold the money? How much money should you hold? How accurately can you forecast an opportunity for a profitable investment? There are several possible solutions. For example, your speculative funds could be kept in interest-bearing accounts at depository institutions or in a money market mutual fund where your money is available upon demand. This way, you would earn at least a modest amount of additional income on your money while you awaited that opportunity for a more profitable investment. Keeping abreast of financial developments and monitoring your household budget fairly closely should keep other problems to a minimum.

When the reinvestment rate on a particular financial instrument is lower than the rate you have been getting, you are likely to hesitate on reinvesting in this instrument. This is only natural, because no one wants to receive less income from any source of earnings. In some instances, this hesitation produces a decision to place the investment funds from the maturing instrument in a holding pattern, like the interest-bearing demand accounts described previously. When this is done, however, you should realize that there is no assurance that the rates of interest or yields on various investments will rise in the near future, and that potential interest earnings will be lost by not reinvesting immediately in a financial instrument that pays more than passbook saving rates or rates on money market mutual funds.

Remember: "Safety, Liquidity, Yield, and Taxes"

Although gaining additional income through investments can be crucial to the future of your household—perhaps even to generations to come—you should not forget, ignore, or downplay the basic considerations for an investor: safety, liquidity, yield, and taxes. The order in which these factors are listed is important. As an average wage earner, you can ill afford to lose any part of your current income. Admittedly, one of the principal elements of investment is risk. However, a careful reading of some of the previous chapters should show you how to reduce this risk to practically zero.

According to officials at banks and thrift institutions, those wage earners who invest in financial instruments are well aware of the importance of safety, but often have problems in deciding between liquidity and yield. Some wage earners are willing to forego as much as an additional 3 percent in yield in order to have high liquidity. As one official said, typical wage earners are very concerned about, "being able to get their money if and when they need it." This kind of concern implies that the investing wage earner feels the need to be prepared to meet a possible emergency with the investment funds.

Indeed, an emergency can reach any level of seriousness in terms of the need for funds. However, one of the factors in an individual's decision about whether he or she is ready to invest is the assurance that a reasonable amount of funds have already been set aside for emergencies. If this provision has been made, the person can invest without being worried about needing his or her money quickly.

We all know that the greater yield on the investment, the more additional income it will generate. On an annual basis, an additional 3 percentage points in yield on a $1,000 investment means an additional $30 in income. While this $30 may not decide whether you will become rich or not, it is money and it can be spent on something you would have had to do without if you hadn't had the $30.

DOING YOUR HOMEWORK

A serious undertaking of personal money management involves both time and effort, but most of this time and effort can be spent right in the home. Such tasks as monitoring the household's cash flow, reading the financial publications, and checking the monthly balances on bank and credit card statements are likely to require some of your time every day. Responsibilities such as reviewing bank and credit card statements are likely to strike you as being boring and tedious. All of these activities, however, are home-centered, and, in the final analysis, all of them should prove to be very valuable in your efforts to attain the highest standard of living possible from your current financial resources.

In addition to monitoring, reviewing, and checking various financial developments, homework in personal money management includes performing certain operations. You must be diligent about maintaining the appropriate financial records and making the hard-nosed decisions needed to enforce the household budget.

Production Minus Consumption Equals Savings

In personal financial management, it is logical to think of your take-home pay as your production, and your actual spending as your consumption. When we subtract consumption from production, the remainder is savings. The ability to save is likely to be the key to your success in personal money management.

You and your family should regard savings as one of the priority expenditures in the household budget. This decision to save should result from a clear understanding by the entire family of the reasons for saving. Such an understanding should make it easier to restrain spending by all members of the household. As the member of the household with training in personal money management, you should initiate and lead this discussion on treating savings like other household expenditures. This task may require more than a single discussion, and, in fact, the discussion is likely to take place each time a request is made for an optional or questionable expenditure.

Analyzing Financial Developments

In chapter 2, considerable discussion is devoted to the value of having the most up-to-date information on financial developments. You are urged to read the financial section of the daily newspaper as thoroughly as you read other sections of the newspaper. You are also urged to subscribe to one or two business newspapers or magazines, and follow whatever financial news is offered by the broadcast media.

To become efficient in personal money management, you must not only seek up-to-date information on financial developments, but also see how it applies to your own circumstances. You should know how much you have available to invest, when you want the income from an investment available for household spending, whether interest rates are likely to increase or decrease in the very near future, and what alternative opportunities for investment are available. These, along with many other points of personal reference, should come to your mind as you read the information on financial developments, and you should relate each item of information to your own household's needs and desires and your overall financial objectives.

A growing problem for small investors is that the information on financial developments is becoming more complex every day. Many investment instruments, for example, have no fixed rate for a year or several years. Because of recent experiences with very high inflation and wide fluctuations in interest rates, many investments today carry variable yields or variable rates of interest. Thus, while there are more investment opportunities for the small investor, there are also more elements involved in the investments. These elements are often complicated and confusing, and unfortunately, they provide the opportunity for deceptive marketing.

CONFIDENCE, COMFORT, AND SECURITY

In all likelihood you and other wage earners are already practicing some aspects of personal money management. You may not have a formal household budget and you may not compare the balance on one monthly bank statement with the balance on previous monthly statements. Nevertheless, you probably record unconsciously excessive spending by the household during a week or two-week period, and you probably react in some way to a bank balance on a monthly statement that is more or less than the usual amount. One could say that you, the average wage earner, practice personal finance each time you respond to a family member's request for a new expenditure by posing the question, "Where is the money going to come from?"

Because of the intense desire by everyone today to seek an ever-rising standard of living, it is not enough to just practice some of the aspects of personal money management. You will never have all the financial resources to do everything you want to do. However, most of us would be satisfied if we thought we were getting or receiving maximum income from the use of both our physical and financial resources. Learning and practicing personal money management can assure maximum income from our financial resources. In the final analysis, this maximum income will mean much more than an increased ability to buy and to enjoy more worldly goods and services. It will generate greater confidence in your power to determine your own destiny. And it will surely provide both you and the members of your household with more security in the future.

Glossary

Accrued interest: interest earnings accumulated on a financial interest-bearing asset.

Adjusted gross income (AGI): gross income (total income) minus any allowable adjustments to income.

Affinity credit card: a card issued by a nonbank group or organization to its members, in an arrangement with a bank.

Agencies: securities issued by such federal agencies as the Federal Land Banks, Federal National Mortgage Association, Government National Mortgage Association, and the Tennessee Valley Authority.

Aggressive growth stock fund: a mutual fund in which the portfolio of securities consists mostly of stocks that are expected to appreciate in value in the very near future.

All-signature account: an account owned by two or more persons arranged so that signatures of all joint owners are required for transactions.

Amortize: to reduce a debt through regular and equal payments.

Annual percentage rate (APR): the cost of credit over a full year, expressed as a percentage, reflecting all costs of the loan as required by the Truth in Lending Act.

Annual rate: the rate of interest to be paid over a full year.

Annual yield: the interest rate paid over a full year compounded.

Annuity: a guaranteed income for life, with payments received at regular intervals; a type of investment offered by insurance companies.

Appreciation: a term synonymous with price improvements or advance—a major objective of investment.

Arbitration: an agreement between two parties that a dispute will be settled by a third party, and that the decision of the third party will be binding on both disputants.

Arrears: amount due and unpaid.

Assets: any owned properties or rights that are available for the payment of an obligation. They include cash and readily marketable securities held as investments, other items considered the equivalent of cash, accounts receivable, merchandise inventory, etc.

ATM: abbreviation for automated teller machines, which are computer-controlled terminals located on bank premises or elsewhere, through which customers of financial institutions make deposits, withdrawals, or other transactions as they would through a bank teller.

Auction: the sale of Treasury securities by the U.S. Treasury on a bid basis.

Balance sheet: a statement showing the nature and amount of a company's assets, liabilities, and capital on a given date.

Balloon payment: a large extra payment that may be charged at the end of a loan or lease.

Banker's acceptances: future claims on a bank backed by the bank's customer; they enable the bank to finance the customer's business transactions, such as a shipment of goods by a third party.

Bankruptcy: an individual's status in which a state law usually allows the individual's creditors to claim his or her assets for repayment of debts (with certain assets or a portion thereof excepted).

Bearer bond: a bond that does not have the owner's name registered on the books of the issuing company or on the bond. Interest and principal are payable to the holder. Endorsement is not required on transfers.

Blue chip companies: large and fairly stable companies that have demonstrated consistent earnings and usually have long-term growth potential.

Bond: a special kind of promissory note that represents the issuer's pledge to pay back the principal on a certain date of maturity, at face value. Until that date, the issuer promises to pay an amount of money, usually every six months, at a fixed rate that is determined when the bond is issued. Unlike a stockholder, a bondholder does not share in profits or losses of the issuer or take part in business decisions.

Book-entry form: a way of recording ownership of Treasury securities, in which the Treasury merely establishes an account in the name of the buyer of the securities. The purchaser receives a receipt and a statement of account.

Brokerage house: a firm, often a member of a stock exchange, that handles the public's orders to buy and sell securities. The firm charges a fee for this service.

Buying on the margin: buying stock by making a down payment instead of paying the full price of the stock. The down payment is expressed as a percentage of the full price and is set by the Federal Reserve Board.

Call feature: the right of an issuer of bonds to retire the debt prior to maturity.

Call protection: the specific period of time during which a callable securities issue cannot be recalled.

Call provision: a provision which gives its holder the option to buy stock at a fixed price within a specified length of time from the writer or seller. Calls are purchased by those who think the stock price may rise.

Callable bonds: a provision in a bond document that gives the issuer the right to buy back the bonds from holders at the face amount before the date of maturity.

Capital gain: a gain or profit derived from the sale or exchange of a capital asset.

Cash management account: a form of investment offered by larger brokerage firms and investment companies.

Ceiling interest rate: the maximum rate of interest allowed by law or official regulations.

Certificate of deposit (CD): a form of time deposit issued by depository institutions that cannot be withdrawn before a specified maturity date without being subject to an interest penalty.

Checking account: a deposit account upon which checks can be written to withdraw funds.

Closed-end: companies in which there is a set number of shares which are to be sold, and are outstanding. The shares are traded on the major exchanges.

Closing costs: fees payable immediately before you receive title to your home. These fees include costs associated with the attorney, preparing and filing the mortgage, taxes, title search, credit report, survey, insurance, etc.

Collateral: something of value pledged to assure repayment of a loan and subject to seizure if the loan is not repaid.

Collateral trust bond: a bond that is secured by financial assets, such as notes receivable and accounts receivable.

Co-maker (or co-signer): an individual with a good credit rating who signs the note of another person to provide additional security for that person's loans.

Commercial paper: short-term, unsecured promissory notes (IOUs) issued by well-known and well-regulated business firms.

Commission: the broker's fee for handling a stock transaction.

Commodities market: a market in which there is active trading of twenty-five or so commodities, many of which are agriculture products such as corn, cotton, and soybeans. The commodity itself is not traded. What *is* traded are contracts for the future delivery of these products.

Common stocks: securities representing an ownership interest in a corporation and carrying specified rights for the owner.

Competitive bid: an offer to buy Treasury securities in which the prospective purchaser states the rate of interest or yield that he or she is willing to accept.

Composite return: dividends plus expected appreciation.

Compounded interest: interest earned on interest already paid on the invested principal when it is left to accumulate with the principal.

Compounding: computing the new principal figure by using as a base both the previous principal and change accruing to that previous principal.

Consumer-type certificate: a certificate of deposit with no federal minimum denomination, issued by depository institutions for periods of from three months to five years.

Contingent monetary receipts: money or income that an individual may or may not receive, depending on future developments.

Corporate bonds: interest-bearing debt instruments or IOUs issued by a business corporation.

Coupon bond: a bond with interest coupons attached. Coupons are clipped as they come due and are presented by the holder to the paying agent for payment of interest.

Coupon interest rate: the interest rate specified on a bond certificate and on interest coupons attached to a bond.

Coupon yield: the interest rate specified on the securities (notes or bonds). This is also referred to as the coupon rate.

Credit: the promise to pay in the future in order to buy in the present.

Credit history: the record of how a person has borrowed and repaid debts.

Credit scoring history: a statistical system used to rate credit applicants according to various characteristics related to credit-worthiness.

Creditor: one who lends money or permits another person to owe money to him or her.

Cumulative: a feature of a preferred stock indicating that if dividends are not paid in full, the accumulations must be paid in the future before any dividends can be paid on the common stock. When stock is noncumulative, the corporation is not obligated to make up unpaid dividends.

Debenture: an unsecured, long-term certificate of debt issued by a company against its general credit rather than against a specific asset or mortgage.

Debit card: a plastic card, similar in appearance to a credit card, that customers may use to make purchases through a point of sale terminal. The machine-readable card allows immediate withdrawal from the customer's checking or savings account with the money being transferred to the merchant's account.

Debt service: interest requirements plus stipulated payments of principal on outstanding debt.

Default: failure to perform a contract obligation, particularly the payment of principal or interest on a bond or note at a stated date.

Delinquent: a debtor who is behind in making payments on a debt and has made no satisfactory arrangement with the lender.

Depository institutions: commercial banks, savings and loan associations, mutual savings banks, savings banks, and credit unions.

Direct deposit: a system in which the employee's or investor's earnings are deposited directly to his or her account at a depository institution.

Discount: a bond selling below par.

Discount a note: the lender deducts the interest amount from the face value of the note and remits the remainder to the borrower.

Discount loan: a loan in which there is a deduction from principal for interest and finance charges at the time a loan is made.

Discount rate: the rate of interest that Federal Reserve banks charge financial depository institutions that wish to borrow funds from these banks.

Discounted price: the actual dollar amount that the purchaser pays for a Treasury bill. The difference between this discounted price and the face value of the bill—assuming the bill is held to maturity—is called the discount.

Disposable income: take-home pay or net pay.

Diversification: spreading investments among different companies and institutions in different fields.

Dividend rate: the annual rate of interest paid on passbook savings accounts.

Dividend yield: percentage earning on stocks that can be computed by simply dividing the annual dividend by the market price of the stock.

Dividends: earnings on the ownership of stock, both common and preferred.

Dow-Jones industrial average: number indicators of the movements of prices of certain groups of thirty stocks (utilities, industrials, transportation, and composite) on the New York Stock Exchange.

Durable goods: manufactured products capable of long use, such as refrigerators, automobiles, and various household appliances.

Early withdrawal penalty: a fee that the depositor must pay in order to withdraw funds from the certificate of deposit before its maturity.

Equities: common or preferred stock in a corporation.

Estate: a person's ownership and/or interest in all forms of property. Also, the financial resources and personal assets left upon the person's death.

Eurodollar: deposits denominated in U.S. dollars at banks and other financial institutions outside the United States.

Executor: an individual appointed in a will and approved by a probate court to administer the disposition of an estate according to directions in the will.

Face value: for insurance, face value is the dollar value that expresses coverage limits. It appears on the front of the policy. For a bond, the value that appears on the face of the bond, the amount the issuing company promises to pay at maturity. It is not an indication of market value.

Family of funds: a number of mutual funds managed by the same investment company, with each fund specializing in a different kind of security or investment product.

Finance charge: the cost of a loan in dollars and cents as defined by the Truth in Lending Act. The interest charged is just one component of the finance charge.

Financial instrument: any written document or contract having monetary value or showing a monetary transaction.

First mortgage: a legal instrument that gives a creditor a claim against an owner's right in real property prior to a claim of all other creditors.

Fixed expenses: expenses such as monthly rent or mortgage payments that must be paid at regular intervals, in set amounts, and do not vary with activity.

Fixed rate certificate of deposit: a certificate of deposit on which the annual interest rate is contractually fixed until maturity.

Float: checkbook money that for a period of time appears on the books of both the check writer and the check receiver due to the normal lag in the check collection process.

Foreclose: a creditor sells property in the possession of the debtor with a view toward applying the proceeds to the liquidation or reduction of the debt.

Garnishee: a legal action taken by a creditor to secure payment of a debt by attaching the debtor's salary or other income.

General obligation bonds: government bonds secured by the full faith, credit, and taxing power of the issuing unit.

"Ginnie Maes": a name given to certificates issued by the Government National Mortgage National Association, a federally-chartered corporation.

Governments: a term given to all securities issued by the U.S. Treasury.

Grace period: the period between the date an item is charged on credit or a billing is received, and the date that interest charges begin.

Growth: appreciation or increase in value.

Hedge: protection against a potential investment loss by making a counter-balancing transaction.

Home equity: the difference between the fair market value of your home and your outstanding mortgage balances.

Impulse buying: unplanned buying or buying on a sudden decision.

Income maintenance programs: government programs that provide financial assistance to people who need a supplement to their income.

Income stock fund: a mutual fund in which the portfolio consists mostly of stocks noted for producing generous dividends.

Inflation: a period of persistent rises in the general price level.

Installment loan: a loan repaid in two or more payments made at regular intervals over a period of time.

Institutional investor: a purchaser or seller of securities who acts on behalf of an institution, such as a pension fund, trust fund, mutual fund, or insurance company.

Interest rate: the price in percentage form paid for credit on the privilege of borrowing money.

Inventory: a completed listing of all the household's assets.

Investment trusts: any firm that takes its capital and invests it in other companies.

Joint tenancy with right of survivorship account: an account owned by two or more persons arranged so that if one joint tenant dies, the surviving tenants continue to have the same rights to the account as they had previously.

"Junk bonds": "high yield," low grade bonds that are rated as speculative by the major rating agencies, and are therefore considered more risky than high- or investment-grade bonds.

Leveraging: the act of buying income-producing assets such as stocks, bonds, or real estate with a relatively modest amount of the buyer's own funds and a significant amount of funds from other sources.

Liquid assets: all real and personal property owned by a person or household that can easily be converted into cash at a readily determinable fair price.

Liquidity: the ease with which an asset can be converted into cash with little risk of loss of principal.

Loan provision: a clause in the policy that explains how the policyholder can borrow up to the total accumulated cash value of the policy.

Logo: a symbol used by a particular firm or agency for identification purposes.

Long-term capital gain: a gain made on the buying and selling of a capital asset held for more than one year.

Low-grade, high-yield bonds: bonds issued by corporations who are able to obtain from the major rating agencies ratings that would attract most investors.

Margin call: a demand from a broker to repay part of a loan used to help purchase stock—if the value of the stock falls below a certain percentage of the outstanding loan amount.

Margin on mortgage loans: the number of percentage points the lender adds to the index rate to determine the interest rate to be charged.

Margin rate: the proportion of the total purchase price of securities that must be paid in cash.

Marginal tax rate: the tax rate applicable to the highest portion of one's taxable income.

Market-makers: brokers who are willing to buy back a security from a customer at a certain price.

Market rate: average rate of interest set by the major suppliers and users of credit.

Maturity: the date when the debt is due.

Maturity yield: the rate of return expressed in a percentage that will be obtained on an investment if the investment is held to maturity.

Minimum denomination: smallest amount you can buy.

Money market assets: investments in financial instruments such as bank certificates of deposit and short-term Treasury securities.

Money market CD: a certificate of deposit purchased from a depository institution. The minimum denomination is $2,500 and the maturity or term is 26 weeks.

Money market investments: investments that yield the market rate of interest as money market deposits accounts and money market mutual funds.

Mortgage bond: a bond secured by real estate.

Municipal bonds: interest-bearing obligations of a state or any political subdivision of a state, such as a town, county, or city.

Mutual funds: registered investment companies whose securities are offered to the public and whose assets are invested in a number of different securities in which the shareholders have, in effect, an undivided interest.

Net equity: total market value of the securities in the investor's account less any outstanding loans or fee charges on the account.

Net worth: the difference between the assets and debts (liabilities) of a person or household.

Net worth statement: a financial form that lists, as of a specific date, the financial assets and liabilities of a person or household, and shows the difference between the two as the net worth.

Noncompetitive bid: an offer to buy Treasury securities, in which the prospective purchaser does not state the rate of interest or yield that he or she is willing to accept.

NOW (Negotiable Order of Withdrawal) account: an interest bearing account on which checks may be drawn.

One-signature account: an account owned by two or more persons arranged so that either joint owner is authorized to conduct transactions.

Open-end: companies in which new shares of the fund are sold whenever there is a request.

Opportunity cost: the benefit foregone (or opportunity lost) by using an asset in a particular venture other than its best alternative use.

Optimum value: not always the highest rate of return, but a respectable rate of return, in view of other desirable characteristics, such as safety, liquidity, and minimum tax liability.

Option: the right to buy or sell something at a specified price within a specified period of time.

Optional negotiability: the choice of letting the owner of the certificate transfer it to another person through the proper endorsement.

Overdraft: a check written by a depositor for more money than the depositor has in his or her account.

Overdraft checking: a checking account associated with a line of credit that allows a person to write checks for more than the actual balance in the account, with a finance charge on the overdraft.

Overdrawing an account: writing a check for more than the balance on deposit in the account.

Par value: the face value printed on common and preferred stocks and bonds. As this is meaningless for common stock, most of this stock is issued as no-par stock of one-dollar par.

Passbook savings account: a savings account in which the saver has a book to record all transactions, such as deposits, withdrawals, and interest earnings.

Passive activity: any activity that involves the conduct of any trade or business, and in which the taxpayer does not materially participate. Any rental activity is considered a passive activity even if the taxpayer does materially participate in the activity.

P/E ratio: price/earnings ratio; expressed as a multiple of the price of a share of stock to the company's earnings per share.

Petition: a written request to a court or a judge asking the granting of some remedy or relief.

Point of Sale (POS): Point of sale systems allow for transfer of funds between accounts, authorization for credit, verification of checks and provision of related services at the time of purchase. POS terminals are located in some shopping areas and allow customers of participating financial institutions to effect transactions through the use of machine-readable debit cards.

Points: additional fees that may be charged in home equity loans and are often collected at closing; a point is equal to one percent of the amount financed.

Portfolio: the aggregate of investments held by an individual or organization.

Preferred stock: corporate ownership that features a fixed dollar income. If the corporation has any earnings, this form of ownership has a claim on earnings and assets before the claim of common stock.

Premium bonds: bonds selling above par.

Prime rate: interest rate charged by commercial banks to their most credit-worthy customers. It is a minimum rate and it takes into account the customer's deposit balance and financial strength.

Principal: the total amount borrowed originally, or the face amount of the loan.

Proceeds of the policy: the total amount of the insurance policy realized or to be received by the beneficiary when the policy is paid off.

Project bonds: municipal obligations, with maturities longer than one year, backed by the federal government.

Project notes: municipal obligations, with one-year maturities, backed by the federal government.

Prospectus: a document issued by a company and filed with the Securities and Exchange Commission to describe the securities to be offered for sale and under what conditions they will be offered, as well as the prospects for company performance.

Rate: a percentage of the principal; the fixed interest that the issuer or borrower promises to pay you for using your money.

Rating organizations: firms that operate investment advisory services. The firms evaluate the relative worth of particular securities.

Real income: an individual's income in dollars adjusted for a change in the price level.

Redeem: to buy back.

Regional exchanges: any organized securities exchange outside New York City.

Registered bond: a bond in which the owner's name is registered with the paying agent. The paying agent is a commercial bank that distributes the interest payments and repayment of principal.

Remaining liquid: having assets in cash or in a form that can be converted to cash immediately and easily.

Repurchase agreements: agreements by a bank or the Federal Reserve to buy back, under certain terms, securities that it originally sold to a second party.

Returned check: a check submitted by a depositor to his or her bank for payment but returned unpaid for one reason or another.

Revenue bond: bond for which the interest and return of principal is payable from and secured by stated and expected revenues from a specific project or group of projects.

Round lot: the general unit of trading in a security, such as 100 shares.

Savings instrument: any contractual agreement with a financial institution in which the saver is assured of interest earnings on his or her funds.

Securities Exchange Commission (SEC): the federal agency charged with the responsibility of regulating the securities market and all publicly held investment companies.

Second mortgage: a loan specifically secured by an individual's equity in real property, which is subordinated to the equity interests of any first mortgage holder.

Secondary market: a market for buying and selling previously issued securities.

Secured bond: a bond secured by tangible assets.

Short-selling: a technique in which an investor borrows stock from a broker in the hope of selling it on the market when the price of the stock is high, then buying it back when the price has dropped, and returning it to the broker after having made a profit.

Short-term: a period of one year or less.

Signature loan: a loan granted on the basis of a borrower's credit worthiness and signature; not secured by collateral.

Simple interest: a method of calculating interest on the outstanding balance that produces a declining finance charge with each payment of the installment loan.

Sinking fund: a reserve of cash set aside annually from corporate earnings to ensure that there will be enough money to redeem bonds at maturity.

Speculative venture: an investment made despite great uncertainty in the hope of making a profit or achieving a substantial gain.

Split rate: an interest rate structure that pays regular NOW account rate on the first $2,500 and a much higher rate on the account balance above $2,500.

Statute of limitations: a law which bars suits upon valid claims after the expiration of a specified period of time.

Statutes: laws established by the acts of a legislature.

Stock certificate: evidence of ownership of stock in the form of a certificate, which shows, among other things, the number of shares owned, the issuing corporation, whether the stock is at par value, and the rights of the stockholder.

Stop payment: a request by a depositor to his or her bank to refuse payment on a check written by the depositor.

Sweep: an operation in which a depository institution periodically removes funds from one account of a depositor and places such funds into a higher-yielding account for the depositor.

Tax avoidance: the use of legal means to minimize one's taxes.

T-bills: short-term U.S. Treasury securities issued in minimum denominations of $10,000 and usually having initial maturities of three, six, or twelve months.

Tender: a form used to purchase Treasury bills.

Term: the length of time for which the principal is borrowed.

"Thrifts": a general term for savings and loan associations, credit unions, mutual savings banks, and savings banks.

Time deposits: funds that are deposited under agreement for a stipulated period of time.

Title: evidence that a person is the legal owner of property.

Transactions account: any account on which checks are written regularly to pay bills.

Transfer agent: a firm, typically a bank, that is authorized by a corporation to administer and record the transfer of its stocks or bonds between investors.

Treasury notes: intermediate-term, coupon-bearing U.S. Treasury securities having initial maturities of from two to ten years and issued in denominations of $1,000 or more.

Treasury securities: interest-bearing obligations of the U.S. government issued by the Treasury Department. These obligations fall into three categories—bills, notes, and bonds.

Variable annuity: an annuity contract providing lifetime retirement payments that vary in amount with the results of investment in a separate account portfolio.

Variable rate: an interest rate that changes periodically in relation to an index. Payments may increase or decrease accordingly.

Variable rate certificate: a savings certificate on which the rate of interest payable changes, depending on the term for which the money is pledged.

Vendors: companies that sell.

Volatility: a measure of the rapidity with which a security changes in value as compared to the market generally.

Yield (or rate of return): measurement of the profitability of an investment; it is usually per year on the amount invested; often referred to as return on investment.

Zero coupon bond: a bond that pays no interest. It is sold at a deep discount at the time of issuance; thus the buyer's gain is the difference between the discount price and the face value of the bond collected at maturity.

Source Notes

Chapter 1

1. *Richmond Times-Dispatch*, June 9, 1987.
2. *Richmond Times-Dispatch*, June 26, 1987, p. E-3.
3. *Richmond Times-Dispatch*, June 24, 1987, p. E-1.
4. *Richmond Times-Dispatch*, June 28, 1987, p. E-1.
5. *Richmond Times-Dispatch*, July 20, 1984, p. B-3.

Chapter 2

1. *Washington Post*, July 16, 1987, p. E-3.
2. *Ibid.*

Chapter 12

1. Steven H. Chapman, Mitchell P. LaPlante, and Gail Wilensky, "Life Expectancy and Health Status, the Aged," *Social Security Bulletin*, vol. 49, no. 10 (October 1986), p. 44.
2. *Richmond Times-Dispatch*, March 16, 1987, p. E-3.

Index

DATE DUE

APR 1 6 1989		
MAR 9 1990		
ILL 2-19-93		
MAY 0 5 1993		
DEC 1 4 1996		
JUL 0 5 '98		